Anthropological Studies of Human Fertility

Anthropological Studies of Human Fertility

edited by Bernice A. Kaplan

Wayne State University

WAYNE STATE UNIVERSITY PRESS · DETROIT 1976

Most of these studies were presented at the Symposium on Anthropological Aspects of Fertility at the annual meeting of the American Association for the Advancement of Science, in New York on January 27, 1975. They are reprinted from Human Biology, *volume 48, number 1, 1976.*

Library of Congress Cataloging in Publication Data
Main entry under title:

Anthropological studies of human fertility.

"Most of these studies were presented at the Symposium
on Anthropological Aspects of Fertility . . . in New York
on January 27, 1975. They are reprinted from Human
biology, volume 48, number 1, 1976."
    Includes bibliographies.
    1. Fertility, Human—Addresses, essays, lectures.
2. Medical anthropology—Addresses, essays, lectures.
I. Kaplan, Bernice A., 1923-   II. Symposium on
Anthropological Aspects of Fertility, New York, 1975.
III. Human biology.
GN241.A48   301.32'1   76-2663

ISBN 0-8143-1558-5

Contents

v

Introduction

Concern with population growth and the devising of social, economic and other devices for the control of human population growth have been with man from early times, although the formal literature in this area is of much more recent vintage. When population pressures became too concentrated in certain of the Pacific Islands (Tikopia, among others) the elders would send out boatloads of youths on journeys from which it was known they would never return. In this manner they would win for those remaining the possibility of a balance between the productive capacity of the environment and the population demands upon the territory for succeeding years. Long before Planned Parenthood and Zero Population Growth, societies were instituting social practices to limit population growth.

Census enumerations of population size have been part of human history since the time of the early city-states, where counts were made for taxation purposes, for military levys and to know how many potential laborers were available within the city boundaries. Within recent centuries these data have been analysed in increasing detail—frequently for the same purposes, although such goals are often hidden by circumlocution. Densities have been plotted per room, per household, per city block, per urban (or rural) area, per nation, and—most recently—in terms of population pressure on spaceship Earth.

Anthropologists, however, have begun to bring a slightly different perspective to the analysis of demographic data, and it is this new approach that the papers in this symposium represent. The data used by the anthropologist comes from circumscribed, boundaried communities, usually intimately known to the researcher. In this framework the investigator is often able to recognize influences on fertility and fecundity which the demographer, used to working with national samples (or censuses), may be less cognizant of, primarily because his data are so often divorced from the social reality within which these influences have their reality. These anthropological demographic studies have expanded only recently and the time is not yet ripe for a comprehensive survey of the generalizations achieved. Perhaps not surprisingly, some few of the anthropological findings, even now, replicate observations made earlier by other researchers. Since independent verification is one measure of scholarly accuracy this testing by different methods on different material should be seen as significant. Furthermore, some of the questions posed by anthropologists in studies of small scale may be amenable to testing in larger sized samples. Lastly there are purely anthropological demographic questions applicable only to the types of populations being studied. The time now seems ripe for exploring the chief classes of study by collecting together the results of representative anthropological studies.

HISTORY

With the increasing awareness of a world population crisis, evident in a growing body of scholarly and popular literature; with action groups organized to work toward reduction in the rate of population increase; and, of course, with growing research interest in this area of concern, anthropologists characteristically began to investigate populations and the variety of factors which influence their expansion (and occasional contraction). In 1973 Section H (Anthropology) of the American Association for the Advancement of Science agreed to serve as sponsor for a series of studies on population and means of population control in selected areas of the Third World. The Research Institute for the Study of Man has continued to advance these studies. In the summer of 1973, prior to the International Congress of Anthropological and Ethnological Sciences, Dr. Sol Tax brought together a body of world anthropologists concerned with anthropological aspects of world population growth to devise strategies for the education of people in areas of high population pressure concerning the possibility of limiting population growth and improving living conditions.

1974 was World Population Year during which time many symposia, international conferences, position papers and policy pronouncements were forthcoming. It was a period of intensified attention to population problems, and as such, tended to stimulate interest in expansion of available data bearing on questions related to population density and to the carrying capacity of the earth. As a measure of the increasing interest in these topics, at least two events in which the principal participants were biological anthropologists took place in 1974. At the annual meeting of the American Association of Physical Anthropologists (April, 1974, Amherst, Massachusetts) 15 papers on demographic topics were submitted for the program. During August of that year there was an International Workshop on Demographic Aspects of Human Biology at Erice, Sicily, organized by Gabriel Lasker and Brunetto Chiarelli, and supported by grants from the National Science Foundation and NATO division of scientific affairs. This workshop brought together both fully professional researchers and advanced graduate students to share their research interests and concerns. Participants came from a wide portion of the earth's surface: from Latin and North America, from Great Britain, Scandinavia, the Netherlands, Poland, Hungary, Germany, Belgium, France, Portugal, Italy, Yugoslavia,

Czechoslovakia, Iran and India. Their interests ranged from paleodemography to theoretical population genetics, from lactation to starvation as controls of population, from the examination of past theories to the development of new ones.

There are a limited variety of ways in which populations may increase or decrease: births, deaths, immigration and emigration. As medical knowledge comes to be generally available deaths have been decreasing and, laudable as this is, it does mean that more people are around for a much greater period of time not only to produce and reproduce, but also to consume. Migration too has profound local effects (as well as on the genetic make-up of the donor and receiving populations). Obviously this only serves to shift the concentration of people and has no effect on the numbers of the species as a whole, however. Thus, fertility is the key variable.

With these thoughts in mind, and as Chairp of Section H of the AAAS responsible, among other things, for program development, I asked Lasker, who had expressed an interest in doing so, to organize a symposium on anthropological studies of fertility for the 1975 meeting to be held in New York City—a session which would be jointly sponsored by the American Association of Physical Anthropologists. Since relatively few Americans were to be represented at the workshop at Erice, Sicily which he was then in the midst of organizing, he indicated his willingness also to organize a symposium in America devoted to the problems and results of studies of fertility by anthropologists. The emphasis was to be on biological anthropology to limit the scope since only one half-day session was available for the program. The numerous socio-cultural factors could thus only be considered as they impinge on human population biology. In fact, other sessions at the same meetings were devoted to the socio-cultural aspects of population growth.

As the date for the symposium approached, Lasker became temporarily incapacitated (by the bane of improperly evolved Homo, a so-called slipped disc—apparently related to an imperfect evolutionary adaptation to erect posture), and I volunteered to chair the session and to edit the symposium. One of the participants did not prepare his presentation for publication and this has made room in this publication to expand the symposium further by including one article prepared for the meeting but not presented there and two other papers which take more account of socio-cultural factors and make the range of topics more representative of the title "Anthropological Studies of Fertility."

Physical anthropology is attempting to see population growth not only in terms of analysis of census materials but, through in situ studies of the dynamics of population growth, to develop additional insights and understandings of population changes. (For example, for several decades many sociologists were concerned by the number of city blocks which separated the residences of future mates as a measure of population mobility. Goeffrey Harrison and his colleagues, working through three centuries of parish records of the towns of Oxmoor in Oxfordshire determined that the maximum distance from which most new genetic material would be brought into the community could be measured by the distance which a courting swain could comfortably walk there and back in one day.) Other anthropologists, including Derek Roberts who studied the population of Tristan da Cunha, an island in the middle of the South Atlantic, have concerned themselves with inbreeding and population growth. Biological anthropologists tend to go beyond the theory of demographic transition (with its reliance on the changed population pyramid associated with the shift from subsistence to surplus economies (including industrialization), by seeking different responses to population pressures (ranging from disease agents to systems of inheritance, from infant mortality to varying systems of family residence). All of these, and ecological stresses as well, have their effects on the world population structure.

The papers in this symposium represent these interests. Kunitz and Slocumb examine differential utilization of surgical procedures for abortion and sterilization as a means of control of reproduction among Navajo and Hopi Indians of the American Southwest, and posit a relationship between the observed rates and the opportunities for contact and interaction with the dominant society. Friedl and Ellis examine the impact of inheritance patterns, limited ecological opportunities, and the practice of late marriage and celibacy on the population structure of an isolated village in a closed valley in Switzerland. As rural industrialization provides new opportunities for economic support older patterns break down: outmigration and exogamy increase, the age at marriage decreases as does the size of the completed family.

In population genetics random genetic drift applies only to small populations and has no impact on large ones—in which other evolutionary forces predominate. Masnick and Katz demonstrate that in demography also the ideal statistical models used for large populations are not the ones needed for small populations. The appropriate models for small circumscribed populations are still not well developed. Their paper also presents a challenge to traditional demographic transition theory in that they show that among the Eskimo population in Barrow, Alaska fertility is not controlled by late marriage and high infant mortality. The reproductive rate is related to the economic status of the community at the time childbearing began such that higher fertility is shown by women who began childbearing in times of prosperity in contrast to those who began their families during times of economic hardship.

Liberty, Hughey and Scaglion examine one of the accepted beliefs concerning declining birth rates associated with migration from rural to urban environments and find that the new urbanite Omaha Indian woman desires, not fewer, but more offspring than do her reservation-bound counterparts. These desires are expressed in actual production of larger families. These authors find an absence of negative attitudes toward use of birth control methods, nor is there ignorance of the "available technology." Liberty and her co-workers suggest that their findings may be related either to the recency of the urban experience or to the realities of their participation in the welfare state.

Hesser, Blumberg and Drew note a change in sex ratio associated with the presence of the Hepatitis B surface antigen in the blood of the parents. Though the difference in sex ratio is not statistically significant in any of the Melanesian populations surveyed, the direction of the difference is similar in all four, an occurrence which has only a .01 chance of occurring "by chance." A similar, but slightly different effect on sex ratio had previously been encountered in a Greek population. Obviously, such changes in sex ratio, associated with disease vectors (and the authors suggest the possibility of similar differences associated with other diseases) will have impact on future population structure, as will any attempt to eradicate the disease.

Abelson looks at another aspect of the ecology, altitude, and measures the effect of hypoxia stress on fecundity and fertility in the Peruvian Andean *altiplano.* He compares reproductive rates in both high and low altitude communities and finds higher fertility at low altitudes: highest among those native to the area, intermediate among those who have lived for a time in the valley community, and lowest in those living in the high sierra. Thus, removal of the stress of hypoxia appears to increase fertility.

Ryder examines the relationship between family residence patterns and fertility in Yucatan. Contrary to other suggestions in the literature, there is a higher rate of fertility among Yucatecans living in nuclear households than among those in households made up of members of extended families. Most of his sample, however, had lived under more than one residence system during their lifetimes, depending on their age, economic position and capacity to support themselves apart from the extended kin. Those living in nuclear family households were better off economically and also somewhat older, hence it was not surprising to find their family size greater.

Frisancho, Klayman and Matos, studying an economically poor population sample from Lima, Peru, concluded that following maternal age, the best predictor of number of live births per mother is the total number of childhood deaths. The increase in childhood deaths leads to an increase in the number of live births as a means of compensation. In this connection one might observe that if children born previously die and are replaced by other offspring there is no increased load on the earth's resources and the only energy drain is on the output of the female.

McAlpine and Simpson, in their comparisons of fertility and other parameters of population structure in two Canadian Eskimo communities, corroborate, at least statistically, some of the findings of Frisancho, Klayman and Matos. In the Eskimo communities, as in Lima, Peru, replacement of offspring (infants and children) who die young occurs at higher frequencies than does the increase of family size where no loss through death is present. McAlpine and Simpson suggest that there is a more rapid replacement of offspring following death of a male child than of a female child. It is important that bodies of data, such as is represented in the Igloolik-Hall Beach comparison, continue to be made available, for ultimately the testing and documenting of new theories and hypotheses will depend on the widest possible variety of information on the population structure of societies of small scale.

Reid's paper reexamines the question of the impact of consanguineous matings on fertility and infant mortality as observed in rural Sri Lanka (Ceylon). His studies reverse the findings of earlier, similarly designed, investigations since his data show a decrease in couple fertility associated with consanguineous matings, but no significant decrease in offspring viability. The relation between closeness of kin ties and matings suggests that Darwinian fitness is indeed better maintained by minimization of consanguinity in marriage.

As the reader will soon note, the interests represented here range from an examination of the cultural aspects of population distribution (Kunitz and Slocum, Friedl and Ellis, Liberty, Hughey and Scaglion) through both the impact of economic stress on birth spacing (Masnick and Katz), and the interaction of disease and sex ratio affecting interrelationships between populations and ultimately genetic variability (Hesser, Blumberg and Drew) to environmental aspects of population growth (Abelson). Other topics include the impact of family residence patterns and inbreeding rates (Ryder and Reid) and the relationship between high mortality and high fertility (Frisancho, Klayman and Matos, as well as McAlpine and Simpson). Anthropological demography is already well diversified despite its young age.

I believe that the interest in demography among anthropologists will continue and hope that research will be stimulated—especially through simultaneously taking into account more of the factors influencing fertility than any one of the present authors has done. Furthermore I believe that the research of other scholars, social anthropologists, demographers and population biologists among them, will be augmented because of what anthropologists have learned concerning a question of mutual interest—the fertility of human populations.

BERNICE A. KAPLAN

Department of Anthropology
Wayne State University
Detroit, Michigan 48202

The Use of Surgery to Avoid Childbearing among Navajo and Hopi Indians[1]

By Stephen J. Kunitz[2] and John C. Slocumb[3]

ABSTRACT

Previous work has shown that Hopis have reduced their fertility much more rapidly than Navajos since World War II. While several methods of birth control are probably used with varying degrees of success, this paper shows that surgical means for averting childbearing appear to play an important role. Abortions are slightly less common among Hopi than Navajo women, but the former have a higher rate in the older age groups. Hysterectomies and bilateral tubal ligations are more common among Hopis. Vasectomies are virtually never done on Hopi and Navajo men.

The Hopi and Navajo Indians have lived as neighbors in Northern Arizona for several centuries but have made very different adaptations to the same setting. Hopis are sedentary agriculturists living in villages on or at the base of three mesas where sufficient water has been available to permit subsistence farming. The village of Moenkopi, 50 miles from the main reservation, was originally a summer farming colony and is now inhabited year round.

By way of contrast, the Navajos are semi-sedentary pastoralists living in scattered family groups on a large reservation surrounding both Moenkopi and the Hopi Reservation. The Navajo population numbers about 130,000 (plus or minus 10%) on reservation in contrast to 5,000 or so reservation resident Hopis. Since the beginning of the reservation period about a century ago, the Navajo population has grown at a faster rate than the Hopi, and we have attributed this to differences in mortality rather than fertility for the period ending shortly after World War II. During that period, fertility in each tribe seems to have been equally high; since then mortality has dropped rapidly for both, but Hopi fertility has declined much more sharply than Navajo.

[1]The work on which this report is based was supported in part by National Science Foundation (RANN) Grant GI-34837 and is contribution number 12 from the Lake Powell Research Project.

[2]Departments of Preventive Medicine and Community Health and of Sociology, University of Rochester, Rochester, N.Y. 14642.

[3]Department of Obstetrics and Gynecology, University of New Mexico, Albuquerque, N.M. 87106.

Elsewhere we have traced some of the differences between these two tribes that we believe have influenced their recent population history (Kunitz 1974a, 1974b). Briefly, we have shown that age specific fertility rates among Hopi women in their 30's and above are much lower than for Navajo women in the same age group. This reduction in Hopi fertility seems to have been due to several factors: greater educational achievement; more rapid entry into wage work; and perhaps cultural differences that are as yet undefined. Finally, the differences in educational level, employment, and emigration between the two tribes seem to be related to the fact that the Navajo Reservation was increased several times by governmental action. This expansion seems to have encouraged a persistence of a subsistence livestock economy on the Navajo Reservation and has until recently allowed a large number of families to live in much greater isolation than was true among the Hopis. On the other hand, the densely settled Hopi villages made them much more accessible to the influence of government agents and missionaries than were the Navajos.

In the present paper we present data for each population which shows differences in the way surgical sterilization and abortion are used. We will not deal with other means of averting childbearing because such information is only available from studies done among Navajos (Wallach, et al. 1967, Bollinger, et al. 1970, Slocumb, et al. 1975). It may be argued that the difference in degree to which each population uses surgical procedures for averting childbearing is really a measure of lack of success with less drastic means. Thus, sterilization may be the method of last resort when pills, loops, or condoms have failed or are considered too risky or unsafe by the users. While that would seem to be a resonable suggestion, it appears to us that considering the previously reported higher birth rate among the Navajos, the Hopis might have a relatively greater intensity of desire to avoid childbearing reflected in a higher rate of use of surgical procedures.

Though fertility control seems to have been exercised in many nonindustrial societies (Polgar 1972), the evidence from ethnographic studies in this century indicates that among Hopis and Navajos, as well as other Southwestern tribes, fertility has been generally high (Hrdlička 1908). Moreover, until the past 10 or 15 years, the Indian Health Service and the Bureau of Indian Affairs were both reluctant to offer family planning services or to do abortions, even when requested by the pregnant woman herself (McCammon 1951). Since the mid 1960's such services have been made increasingly available to American Indians on essentially the same basis as to other segments of the U.S. population (Rabeau and Reaud 1969).

With the growing availability of various methods of contraception, the necessity of surgical procedures for preventing childbearing would seem to be on the wane. Such procedures are still of considerable importance, however, both within Indian populations as well as in the larger U.S. population. Between 1965 and 1970, for instance, there was a considerable increase in the national prevalence of sterilization procedures (Bumpass and Presser 1972), and the same seems to have been true among Navajos (Slocumb et al. 1975) and presumably among Hopis. Nationally, the procedures vary depending on a number of characteristics. Tubal ligations were more frequent among lower status, high parity women, and vasectomies more common among higher status males. We would expect to discover such differences within and between Indian populations as well.

Hibbard (1972) has shown that, at a major teaching hospital, there was a several-fold increase in elective hysterectomies for sterilization purposes over a two and-a-half year period. He has suggested that this was a result of growing enthusiasm on the part of physicians and patients alike, reflecting a willingness to perform or undergo a hysterectomy for what might previously have been regarded as relatively minor symptoms not otherwise justifying such drastic surgery. Further, many hysterectomies were done in the absence of any indications apart from the desire for sterilization.

Therapeutic abortions have also increased in recent years, especially since the passage of more liberal legislation in many areas. In a review of records from a large number of general short-term stay hospitals compiled by the Professional Activity Survey, Tietze (1968) reported the highest rates to be in the West (4/1,000 deliveries) and the Northeast (2.5/1,000). Whites had higher rates than non-whites (2/1,000 versus 1.1/1,000). Locally operated and controlled government hospitals had lower rates than teaching hospitals.

Since the liberalization of abortion laws in the early 1970's, rates have increased substantially from those reported immediately above. Peak rates are found in New York (921 per 1,000 live births) and Washington, D.C. (4,208 per 1,000 live births) in 1973. These rates are elevated by the attraction of women to those areas where the procedure may be more readily obtained. In the three southwestern states where most Navajos and Hopis live, the 1973 rates are as follows: New Mexico, 222; Arizona, 71; and Utah, 4 (Weinstock et al. 1975).

In a New York City teaching hospital, Rovinsky and Gusberg (1967) showed that therapeutic abortions increased between 1953 and 1964, especially for private rather than ward patients. They thought that the disparity was due to the greater sophistication of private patients who were more aware of the various indications for therapeutic abortion, such as rubella, and who received prenatal care beginning earlier in pregnancy when abortions are most commonly performed.

Abortions may have a significant impact on birth rates. For example, in the eight years after the legalization of abortion in Japan the crude birth rate dropped from 34 to 18 per 1,000 (Cox 1970: 380). As other contraceptive measures have become more readily available and more reliable, the frequency of abortions has declined (See also Henry 1973).

It has been implicit in many of the findings reported above that social class and cultural differences are related to the use made of surgical procedures for preventing childbearing. It should not be surprising to discovered such differences between American Indian populations.

METHODS

Our data come from two different sources. First, computer tapes of all discharges from Indian Health Service and contract facilities in the Navajo and Phoenix Area Offices during fiscal years 1972 and 1973 (7/1/71-6/30/72 and 7/1/72-6/30/73). And second, data published by the Commission on Professional and Hospital Activities (1972) for 1971.

The Indian Health Service (I.H.S.) data represent as nearly complete coverage of any population groups as one is likely to find in the United States. There are losses from the system, however, that are accounted for by: 1. the use of facilities such as some mission hospitals which do not have contracts with the I.H.S.; 2. the use of contract facilities where care is paid for by insurance or out of pocket; 3. the failure to seek care at all; and 4. less significant in the present instance, treatment of many problems on an out-patient basis. These are not large enough problems to warrant discarding the information as it is almost certainly the case that the vast majority of Navajos and Hopis make use of the facilities covered by these tapes.

The published data from the Commission on Professional and Hospital Activities (C.P.H.A.) is from the Professional Activity Survey (P.A.S.). We have used the 1971 data from United States Hospitals. These are summary statistics of discharges from about 1,500 general hospitals serving approximately one third of the short-term patients discharged from all such U.S. facilities. The C.P.H.A. has rearranged many of the widely used International Classification of Diseases (ICDA) categories to conform to its own HICDA format (U.S. Dept. H.E.W., 1968). A manual allows for ready conversion from one system to another and makes it possible to reclassify the Indian Health Service data in tables comparable to those from the non-federal hospitals in the P.A.S. network. A major problem with these data, however, is that a patient appears only once for his or her most important diagnosis. Secondary and tertiary diagnoses which may be important in epidemiological investigations may not be retrieved from the published tables. In making comparisons between the I.H.S. and C.P.H.A. data, therefore, we have used only primary diagnoses, whereas when examining some categories in more detail we have used all I.H.S. records regardless of whether the diagnosis was primary, secondary, or tertiary.

RESULTS

The first point to be made is that it does not appear that Navajos and Hopis differ in the degree to which they experience complicated pregnancies and deliveries. We have used the rate of ectopic pregnancies as an indicator, as it is a naturally occurring complication of pregnancy associated with age, parity, history of spontaneous abortion, pelvic infections, infertility, and chronic follicular salpingitis (Kleiner and Roberts 1967). In Table 1 we have displayed the rates per 1,000 pregnancies for both tribes and for the P.A.S. population. Given the small numbers especially of Hopis, it is clear that the rates do not differ in any substantively significant way.

When we dichotomize deliveries into normal, without complications (ICDA 650) versus all complicated deliveries (ICDA 651-662) we find that Hopis and Navajos have about the same rate of uncomplicated deliveries (62.5 and 60.0% respectively) and are both slightly lower than the P.A.S. population (68.7%).

Induced abortions have not been common among American Indians. In Table 2 we have displayed the abortion rates for each tribe and the P.A.S.

Table 1

Ectopic Pregnancies—1st Diagnoses only

	Hopi		Navajo		P.A.S.	
Age	Number	Rate/1,000 Pregnancies	Number	Rate/1,000 Pregnancies	Number	Rate/1,000 Pregnancies
0-19	0	0	2	1.5	481	2.1
20-34	2	6.9	20	3.2	5,111	5.1
35-49	0	0	9	8.0	766	8.5
50	0	0	0	0	3	32.5
Total	2	4.9	31	3.6	6,361	4.7

Table 2
All Abortions—1st Diagnoses only

	Hopi			Navajo			P.A.S.		
Age	Abortions	All 1st Diagnoses Pregnancy & Delivery	Rate/ 1,000	Abortions	All 1st Diagnoses Pregnancy & Delivery	Rate/ 1,000	Abortions	All 1st Diagnoses Pregnancy & Delivery	Rate/ 1,000
0-19	7	102	68.6	107	1,287	83.1	32,151	232,186	138.5
20-34	16	290	55.1	506	6,142	82.3	105,251	1,011,792	104.0
35	6	17	352.9	133	1,112	119.6	18,960	89,439	212.0
Total	29	409	70.9	746	8,541	87.3	156,362	1,333,417	117.3

Table 3

Induced and Spontaneous Abortions per 1,000 Pregnancies, by Age: (primary, secondary, tertiary diagnoses combined)

	Induced		Spontaneous	
Age	Navajo	Hopi	Navajo	Hopi
0-19	53.1	26.3	24.7	35.1
20-39	34.1	34.9	46.7	19.0
40-49	60.9	222.2	55.2	111.1
Total	40.6	40.2	44.4	26.9

population per 1,000 pregnancies. The P.A.S. figures are from Table 153, which combines induced and spontaneous abortions (C.P.H.A., 1972). It is clear that both Indian tribes have a lower rate of abortions of all types than does the P.A.S. population. It is also worth noting that Hopis have a lower over all rate but higher rate in the oldest age group. As this is a combined figure, however, it is important to separate induced from spontaneous abortions. This has been done in Table 3.

The rate of induced abortions per 1,000 pregnancies is virtually identical for each tribe, but the age specific patterns clearly differ. Navajos have a relatively constant rate over all age groups whereas the rate for Hopis rises dramatically in the age group forty and above. This is consonant with the findings reported above that the age specific birth rate declines markedly for older Hopi women.

The overall rate of spontaneous abortions is somewhat lower for Hopis than Navajos though, again, women in the oldest age group have a much higher rate. Combining the rates, we find that a third of pregnancies to Hopi women above the age of 40 are terminated by abortion, either spontaneous or induced. Because the numbers are so small in absolute terms (6 abortions out of 18 pregnancies), there is room for considerable random fluctuation from year to year. The fact that we have only used two years' worth of data may lead one to question whether the pattern is a real one. We will return to this issue below.

There are a variety of sterilizing procedures that may be performed. In the present paper we will consider hysterectomies and bilateral tubal ligations among women and vasectomies among men. Hysterectomies may be performed for purposes other than sterilization. Therefore, in this paper, we have considered only vaginal and abdominal hysterectomies that

Table 4

Vaginal and Abdominal Hysterectomies (all diagnoses)

Age	Hopi			Navajo			Relative Risk Hopi/Navajo
	No.	Pop.*	Rate/ 1,000	No.	Pop.**	Rate/ 1,000	
15-19	0	265	0	3	8,454	0.4	
20-34	7	490	14.3	68	17,716	3.8	3.76
35-49	14	330	42.4	131	9,494	13.8	3.07
50-64	6	274	21.9	20	4,662	4.3	5.09
>65	3	152	19.7	5	2,604	1.9	10.4
Total	30	1,511	19.8	227	42,930	5.3	3.7
Child Bearing Years (15-49)	21	1,085	19.3	202	35,664	5.7	3.4

*Source: estimated from 1968 Bureau of Indian Affairs Census of the Hopi Reservation.
**Source: Bureau of Indian Affairs population register of the Navajo Tribe, 1972.

are not radical procedures: i.e., we have excluded procedures usually done for removal of cancerous lesions. Those included are ICDA codes 69.1, 69.2 and 69.4. The results are presented in Table 4.

Clearly, Hopis have a higher rate at all ages than do Navajos. The fact that the rates are higher even in the age groups when childbearing has terminated would seem to indicate one or more possibilities: 1. there may be a higher incidence of gynecological disease among Hopis; 2. sterilization may not be an important reason for hysterectomy among Hopis at any age; 3. there may be a greater willingness among Hopis than Navajos to define certain conditions as diseases.

Our data do not permit us to deal with this issue definitively. We note, however, that there is a higher rate of diagnosis of prolapse of the uterus among Hopis than Navajos both above and below the age of 44 (See Table 5). Prolapse is usually the result of many child births which serve to weaken the pelvic musculature. The fact that Navajo women tend on the average to have more children than Hopi women (Kunitz 1974b) suggests that they may indeed have a higher prevalence of prolapse but be less willing to undergo surgery to correct it. The reasons behind this decision, if our

Table 5

Primary Diagnosis for Women Having Vaginal and Abdominal Hysterectomies

	Navajo		Hopi	
	Prolapse	Other Diagnoses	Prolapse	Other Diagnoses
Below 44 years	43	102	8	7
45 years and above	22	31	9	4
Total	65	133	17	11

inference is correct, are probably multiple and may include access to medical care, educational level, and cultural values.

Bilateral tubal ligations are specifically sterilizing procedures. In Table 6 we have displayed the age specific rates for each tribe per 1,000 population and per 1,000 pregnancies. The rationale for presenting the rates per 1,000 pregnancies is that over 90% of such procedures were performed on postpartum patients (authors' unpublished data). The indication is that women have the operation done after what they hope is their last pregnancy and are less likely to undergo the operation at other times.

Looking first at the rate of ligations per 1,000 population, it is evident that Hopi women are more likely to be sterilized in their most fertile years whereas above the age of 35 there is no difference between tribes. Not only

Table 6

Bilateral Tubal Ligations

	Navajo				Hopi			
Age	No.	Pop.	Rate/ 1,000 Pop.	Rate/ 1,000 Preg.	No.	Pop.	Rate/ 1,000 Pop.	Rate/ 1,000 Preg.
15-19	6	8,454	0.7	4.2	0	265	0	0
20-34	221	17,716	12.5	33.3	14	490	28.6	44.4
35-49	131	9,494	13.8	107.9	4	330	12.1	222.2
Total	358	35,664	10.0	38.6	18	1,085	16.6	40.2

do Hopi women have higher rates in the 20-34 age group, but they also appear more determined to terminate childbearing when they reach their late 30's and early 40's and are still having children. The Hopi population is small and the numbers involved are therefore subject to considerable random fluctuation. However, the fact that our results are so consistent from one method to another would seem to indicate that the findings are probably not due to chance alone.

In contrast to sterilization procedures on women, those on men are so rare as to be virtually non-existent. In the two year period under consideration, no Hopi men and only 13 Navajo men are reported to have had vasectomies. This may reflect a lack of desire on the part of men, de-emphasis by health educators and lack of medical personnel trained to perform the procedures.

The distribution of operative procedures by place of residence is somewhat difficult to ascertain. However, the 13 Navajo men who had vasectomies all came from the eastern end of the reservation and almost 90% of the women who had tubal ligations came from that area as well. The eastern end of the reservation has been in much more intimate contact with the dominant society than the western end; fertility rates are lower there, involvement in the wage economy is greater, and net rates of out migration are lower (Kunitz 1973, 1974b). In addition, characteristics of the physicians serving each area, particularly in regard to their willingness to perform sterilization procedures, may also serve to explain much of the difference. We have no data on physician characteristics, however, save that trained obstetrician-gynecologists are stationed at hospitals in both areas but not at the Keams Canyon hospital where most Hopis receive their medical care.

DISCUSSION

There is some evidence that Hopi women are more willing than Navajo women to undergo sterilizing procedures. In view of the fact that Hopis tend to be better educated and also to have a lower crude birth rate and lower age specific birth rates in the older age groups, this is not really surprising. Moreover, higher educational attainment may perhaps even influence the degree to which hysterectomies are done for what in the past may have been regarded as a relatively minor cause or at least one which seemed inevitable and therefore not worth doing anything about. Furthermore, accessibility of the hospitals is better for most Hopis than for many Navajos and in itself probably serves to increase utilization.

The fact that vasectomies are very uncommon whereas tubal ligations are relatively more common would seem to reflect some of the same patterns that have been reported for the nation generally. That is, it is women from lower status families who tend to have sterilization procedures whereas it is men from higher status families who have vasectomies. The two Indian populations would appear to be more nearly like other low status populations in this country economically, educationally, and in terms of their fertility related behavior.

There has been considerable feeling on the part of some individuals that the Indian Health Service has engaged in unethical practices in some areas by performing sterilization procedures without informed consent or after exerting undue pressure on patients. Our data concerning Navajo and Hopi Indians does not allow us to make any inferences about the quality of the relationship between patients and providers of care. We can say that abortions appear to occur less frequently among both tribes than among patients served by the hospitals in the P.A.S. system and among the general populations of Arizona and New Mexico. We cannot assert that the same is true concerning tubal ligations because primary operative diagnoses in the I.H.S. records account for fewer than half the cases, the remainder appearing as the second diagnosis. The P.A.S system only gives primary diagnosis and hence the results are not comparable. With abortions, on the other hand, the vast majority of diagnoses in the I.H.S. system were primary and therefore we have felt that comparisons were justified. Whatever the reason, vasectomies are vanishingly rare in each tribe.

It may be suggested that the fact that Hopis have a higher rate of use of surgical procedures simply means that they are less successful than Navajos in using other less drastic means of contraception. As we have not been able to provide comparative data on the use of loops, pills, and condoms in each population, this is a reasonable objection. We believe, however, that the evidence we do have indicates that Hopis are likely to be more successful. First, the lower induced abortion rates among Hopis suggests fewer unwanted pregnancies, presumably due to more successful prevention. Second, data we have presented elsewhere indicate that Navajos are less successful than any other group in their ability to use oral contraceptives. Their success with IUD's is about on a par with most other populations from which data have been published (Slocumb et al. 1975). It seems to us that Hopis would, at worst, have failure rates no greater than those reported for Navajos. Third, the fact that the Hopi crude and age specific fertility rates have been declining over a period of time suggests that other modalities than surgery have also been employed with some considerable degree of success, though what methods are of most significance we cannot determine. Fourth, infant mortality rates may differ enough to create differential incentives for fertility control.

Finally, the rather consistent patterns we have described have not yet been fully explained. Physician characteristics and hospital accessability may account for much. Educational differences may also be significant. Those educational differences themselves are not entirely explained and may be related to differences in cultural values as well as to differences in the degree to which members of each tribe are involved in the wage rather than subsistence economy.

Received: 24 January 1975.

LITERATURE CITED

BOLLINGER, C. C., W. C. CARRIER AND W. J.LEDGER   1970   Intrauterine contraception in Indians of the American Southwest. Am. J. Ob. Gyn. **106**: 669-675.

BUMPASS, L. L. AND H. B. PRESSER   1972   Contraceptive sterilization in the U.S.: 1965 and 1970. Demography, **9**: 531-548.

COX P. R.   1970   Demography. Cambridge University Press, Cambridge, England.

COMMISSION ON PROFESSIONAL AND HOSPITAL ACTIVITIES   1972   Length of stay in PAS hospitals, United States, 1971. Commission on Professional and Hospital Activities, Ann Arbor, Michigan.

HENRY, H. P.   1973   Abortion trends in European socialist countries and in the United States, Am. J. Orthopsychiat. **43**: 376-383.

HIBBARD, L. T.   1972   Sexual sterilization by elective hysterectomy. Am. J. Ob. Gyn. **112**: 1076-1083.

HRDLIČKA, A.   1908   Physiological and medical observations among the Indians of the southwestern United States and northern Mexico, Bureau of American Ethnology, Bulletin 34, U.S. Government Printing Office, Washington, D.C.

KLEINER, G. J. AND T. W. ROBERTS   1967   Current factors in the causation of tubal pregnancy. Am. J. Ob. Gyn. **99**: 21-28.

KUNITZ, S. J.   1973   Demographic change among the Hopi and Navajo Indians. Lake Powell Research Project, Bulletin 2, Institute of Geophysics and Planetary Physics, U.C.L.A., Los Angeles, California.

———   1974a   Factors influencing recent Navajo and Hopi population change. Human Organization, **33**: 7-16.

———   1974b   Navajo and Hopi fertility, 1971-1972. Human Biol. **46**: 435-451.

McCAMMON, C. S.   1951   A study of four hundred seventy-five pregnancies in American Indian women. Am. J. Ob. Gyn. **61**: 1159-1166.

POLGAR, S.   1972   Population history and population policies from an anthropological perspective. Current Anthrop. **13**: 203-211.

RABEAU, E. S. AND A. REAUD   1969   Evaluation of PHS program providing family planning services for American Indians. Am. J. Pub. Hlth. **59**: 1331-1338.

ROVINSKY, J. J. AND S. B. GUSBERG   1967   Current trends in therapeutic termination of pregnancy. Am. J. Ob. Gyn. **98**: 11-16.

SLOCUMB, J. C., C. L. ODOROFF AND S. J. KUNITZ 1975 The use effectiveness of two contraceptive methods in a Navajo population. Am. J. Ob. Gyn. **122**: 717-726.

TIETZE, C. 1968 Therapeutic abortions in the United States. Am. J. Ob. Gyn. **101**: 784-787.

U.S. DEPARTMENT OF HEALTH, EDUCATION, AND WELFARE 1968 Eighth Revision, International classification of diseases, Adapted for use in the United States. P.H.S. Publication 1693 (2 vols.), U.S. Government Printing Office, Washington, D.C.

WALLACH, E. E., A. E. BEER AND C-R. GARCIA 1967 Patient acceptance of oral contraceptives. I. the American Indian. Am. J. Ob. Gyn. **97**: 984-991.

WEINSTOCK, E., C. TIETZE, F. S. JAFFE AND J. G. DRYFOOS 1975 Legal abortions in the United States since the 1973 Supreme Court decisions. Family Planning Perspectives, **7**: 22-31.

Celibacy, Late Marriage and Potential Mates in a Swiss Isolate

By John Friedl[1] and Walter S. Ellis[2]

ABSTRACT

Late marriage and celibacy are discussed as means of reducing population growth in a Swiss Alpine community. These patterns are related to other institutionalized social practices, including inheritance rules and religious beliefs, especially those pertaining to birth control. Recent economic changes are then analyzed with regard to their effects upon these social practices.

Late marriage coupled with a high rate of celibacy can control population by shortening the years of childbearing for women and/or by removing some fecund individuals from the breeding population. Both conscious and unconscious systems of population control are reflected in late marriage and celibacy. Delaying marriage can be a conscious decision to postpone the beginning of childbearing, in the absence of approved or known methods of birth control, and in the presence of values which equate marriage with family.[3] At the same time, factors defining marriagability are often beyond the control of the individual. These affect age at marriage and thus have a definite relation to the rate of fertility of a society.

Examples of social practices which affect age at marriage and the rate of secular celibacy have been documented for European populations, where ecological pressures were strongly felt at an early stage of industrial development. In rural Ireland, the traditional peasant system of inheritance led to late marriage and a high frequency of celibacy. There the entire estate went to one son, usually the eldest; the heir could not marry until his father turned over the estate, frequently creating the anomalous situation of a grown man in his forties without status in his community, called "boy" by his fellow villagers (Arensberg 1937). Sisters were fortunate if they found a husband, but the brothers of the heir were more restricted in their

---

[1]Department of Anthropology, The Ohio State University, Columbus, Ohio 43210.

[2]Department of Anthropology, University of Pennsylvania, Philadelphia, Pennsylvania 19174

[3]Van de Walle (1972:150) suggests that it is unrealistic to expect late marriage to be an effective means of limiting population, and while we tend to agree in general, statements of married female informants indicate the contrary for the village of Kippel, discussed in this paper.

choice—they could stay on the farm as long as they remained single, or they could emigrate, as many of them did in the nineteenth century to the United States, to cities in Ireland and elsewhere in Great Britain, or they could enter the priesthood. In this way the rural population of Ireland was controlled through the combined practices of late marriage, high rate of celibacy, and much emigration.

Like Ireland, Switzerland experienced the pressures of a developing economy and population in a restricted area, but did not experience the mass migration that Ireland saw in the nineteenth and early twentieth centuries; instead, other mechanisms restrained population growth. In this paper we will discuss the problem of population regulation in an isolated mountain valley in the Swiss Alps. Specifically, we will point out how late marriage and celibacy, both on a conscious level and as unconscious results of economic practices in the mountain environment, limited population growth. The data are derived from demographic investigations made by Friedl in 1969-70 and 1972 while conducting ethnographic fieldwork in the village of Kippel, Canton Valais, Switzerland.

THE SETTING

Kippel is one of four communes in a cul-de-sac valley known as the Lötschental. Less than half of the 57 square miles of land in the valley is agriculturally useful. In the traditional agricultural era in the valley's history (roughly from its initial permanent settlement during the Middle Ages until the Second World War), inhabitants lived almost exclusively from a combination of agriculture and dairy farming. Because new land could not be cleared, nor could existing land be used more effectively due to the steepness of the slopes and the barrenness of the soil, population pressure led to a reduced standard of living.

The economy of the Lötschental required extreme specialization in the use of land and buildings. Climatic conditions, coupled with sharp differences in altitude, created vast differences in the fertility of the land in the valley, so that gardens and such crops as potatoes or rye could be grown only in a relatively narrow belt near the valley floor. The rest of the land was used for hay, or for grazing the animals if it was too barren to yield a crop of hay. This situation led to the fragmentation of land holdings into a number of small, dispersed parcels. Such was the case if everyone was to have a viable agricultural holding, for the various kinds of land—garden plots, arable fields, hay meadows and grazing lands—were all necessary, and if one villager held his entire estate in the more fertile lower area of the valley, others would lack the necessary plots for gardens and potato fields (Friedl 1973a).

The fragmentation of land was perpetuated through the practice of partible inheritance, whereby each heir, regardless of age or sex, received an equal portion of the entire estate. Unlike some other variations of partible inheritance, in which the males divide the land and the females receive cash or movable goods, or one male inherits the estate and must compensate the other heirs for their share, the pattern in the Lötschental is complete and equal division of everything in the estate.[4]

Over the years population growth led to the increasing division of estates and the fragmentation of land into even smaller parcels. If the size of the population were not checked, ultimately the amount of land a person inherited would be too small to support a family, and he or she would be forced to emigrate in order to survive. Thus there is a relation between measures of population control and the pattern of inheritance, as well as a direct relation between population growth and migration, in that where land is limited, population must be controlled through low birth rate, high death rate, or emigration.

Endogamy was another factor related to population size and inheritance practices, for both parties in a valley-endogamous marriage could contribute land to the new agricultural operation. In contrast, in valley-exogamous marriages only one spouse would have inherited land in the Lötschental.

From 1900 to 1950 the population of Kippel, the village in the Lötschental from which the primary data were collected, increased from 248 to 363 (46%). At the same time the valley population grew from 999 to

---

[4]Not all alpine valleys have partible inheritance, and it should not be implied that it is the only or the best way of dealing with the problems of terrain and climate. For example, in the Tyrolean valley of Nonsberg, Cole (1971) describes a pattern of impartible inheritance where a single heir inherits the estate. However, in a case where impartible inheritance is the rule, other problems of population regulation arise, in that a relatively larger proportion of the family is disinherited, and may not have the option of eking out a marginal living on a small estate. These problems can be worked out in a number of ways, including the right of the disinherited heirs to remain on the estate as agricultural workers as long as they remain unmarried. Emigration rates are frequently higher in such a situation, where there is no hope of ever acquiring land in one's natal village. We do not mean to imply here that the problem of population regulation stands in simple relationship to the pattern of inheritance—it is a complex problem which we cannot deal with at this time. (For a more complete discussion see Friedl 1974.) However, the pattern of inheritance in the Lötschental did prompt certain parental controls over the marriage of their children, which in turn affected population regulation, as we indicate below.

1412 (41%). Several factors indicate that this growth in population created an economic hardship for the inhabitants of the valley, extending their subsistence needs beyond the capacity of the usable land. At first, the population growth was offset by more intensive use of the land and the use of more marginal land in remote areas of the valley. However, little new land could be cleared, since forests which protect the villages from avalanches could not be converted into fields, and glaciers and rocks limited the expansion of the grazing land and meadows. One direct result of the population increase was to reduce the standard of living; villagers recount the troubled times of the Depression, when there was little to eat and no hope of emigrating. In fact, the return of some out-migrants to farm their small inheritance during the hard times of the 1930s created an even greater problem for those who had remained on the land and taken over their relatives' land in their absence. This hardship was not alleviated until the decade following the Second World War, when a major program of rural industrialization was undertaken in Canton Valais, and many men from the Lötschental took jobs as construction workers and then as laborers in the factories they had built.

In response to population pressure throughout Europe, methods of controlling the growth of population evolved. Both Hajnal (1965) and van de Walle (1972) suggest that during the eighteenth and nineteenth centuries in western Europe there was growing concern over population control. In many countries such concern was translated into law, with the result that

> Legal restrictions on marriage, whether introduced before or after Malthus, created a general atmosphere of restraint, which had to be borne by a large proportion of the population. The older generation was obviously worried by the early marriage of the young (van de Walle 1972:138).

The pattern of late marriage and frequent celibacy in the Lötschental was well established long before population growth became a serious problem there, perhaps in response to the "general atmosphere of restraint" in Western Europe of which van de Walle speaks. These practices apparently became common in the Lötschental in response to the economic pressures of dividing an inheritance among a large number of heirs. However, given the already existing pattern and its potential for population control, as the size of the valley population grew in the late nineteenth and early twentieth centuries, late marriage and celibacy came to be recognized more directly in that capacity. In contrast, the low emigration rate prior to World War II indicates that leaving the valley was not considered a serious alternative method of limiting population in the Lötschental.

RESULTS

Late Marriage and Celibacy

Table 1 indicates the age at marriage for males and females by decade since 1900. Late marriage was strongly related to inheritance practices, for it was customary for parents to wait until they were advanced in years and unable to work the land themselves before turning over use rights to the estate. Thus, if a young person wanted to remain in agriculture and continue residing in the Lötschental, he or she could not marry without parental consent, which carried with it the right to use a portion of the estate. Childbearing was expected to begin immediately after marriage; a couple did not really have the choice of marrying without parental permission and living from the inheritance of one spouse (if indeed that was available), for as the family increased in size, more land would be needed to support it.

Thus the inheritance system enabled the parents, especially the father, to influence the age at marriage of his children. A father could dole out rights to use a portion of the estate to each of his children when he felt they were at an appropriate age. He could also determine to some extent whom they would marry by refusing to give use rights to a child, and making the reason for his refusal clear. The parents also had to consider the results of giving out use rights to the children before they were themselves ready to retire—the more they gave out, the less there was left for their own

Table 1

Mean Age at First Marriage by Sex, Kippel 1900-1969

	Males	Females
1900-09	33.4	27.4
1910-19	32.2	29.7
1920-29	29.9	29.6
1930-39	31.7	29.7
1940-49	30.3	29.1
1950-59	30.1	27.7
1960-69	27.2	26.0

support. Moreover, a cow and a few smaller animals usually went along with rights to use the land, and parents were concerned about the decline in their own standard of living if they were to divest themselves of their livestock.

We consider celibacy, or sexual inactivity, in conjunction with late marriage part of the same decision-making process for both parents and sibling sets. One factor leading to a high rate of celibacy was the delay in marriage itself. The longer the young people were forced to wait until they married, the greater was the likelihood that the engagement would be terminated and not replaced. In addition, parents could apply pressure to prevent a number of their children from marrying by granting use rights to one or two children but not to the others. Thus if both parents survived to age 70, for example, those without use rights, who would probably range in age from 25 to 40, would not have had the opportunity to marry with parental consent. For a woman of 25 to be unmarried is not a problem, but for a woman of 40, whose childbearing years are almost past, the incentive to marry once the estate has been divided is relatively slight. Instead, she is likely to continue residing with her unmarried siblings, pooling the inherited land and buildings and operating a single agricultural unit. And since it was not uncommon for people to survive to 70 and beyond, this pattern occurred frequently in the Lötschental.

Other factors contributed to a high rate of celibacy. For one, there was, and still is, an extremely strong religious tradition dictating chastity for both men and women. The priest literally ruled the valley, and in at least one case his discovery of incontinence led to expulsion from the valley.

Courting patterns also contributed to the practice of celibacy. Traditionally a couple settled as steady sweethearts in their early teens. The courtship lasted for many years, as indicated by the average age of marriage. The couple becomes accustomed to a situation of close friendship and romance without sex, and such a relationship might continue over a period of ten or twenty years. The custom of early and extended relationships between two people long before marriage is possible would seem to produce little pressure to marry. However, a courtship that developed later, say in the early twenties when marriage was more of a possibility, might be expected to produce greater pressure toward an immediate marriage (since sex and procreation would be more closely associated by both parties with the nature of their relationship from the outset). Thus the traditional courting pattern offers a kind of security, in that the boy or girl knows that someone is there waiting, and there is no need to "rush into" marriage.

Another way of enforcing celibacy was an arrangement known as the *Erbgemeinschaft*, or association of heirs. When a group of siblings inherited the parental estate, usually most were single and still living together in one household. They continued to live together as a group until one by one they married and moved into separate households, combining their inheritance with that of their spouses. In some cases, however, there was pressure from the siblings to remain part of their residential unit. The land then was held together and worked jointly, rather than by each individual heir. By stalling on a specific designation of parcels and buildings, the siblings delayed the departure of a brother or sister. Also, by involving each other in the operation of the household economy, there was incentive to remain together. And of course the subtle pressures exerted by siblings in everyday living (such as teasing or nagging) were potentially quite important in making marriage undesirable, and thus in effect forcing celibacy upon those members of the sibship who might not have chosen such a life style for themselves (see Friedl 1973b).

It is one thing to describe a large proportion of the population as unmarried, and quite another to assume a high rate of celibacy. However, in the case of Kippel there are several indications that in fact celibacy, or lack of sexual activity, was a common phenomenon among unmarried individuals in the population. For one, until very recently there was no knowledge of artificial means of birth control, and therefore a good chance that continued sexual activity outside of marriage would result in pregnancy. Even the rhythm method was frowned on by the local priest, who preached abstinence as the most acceptable means of limiting family size.

Late marriage indicates the probability of celibacy, since in the absence of birth control or abortion one expects a large number of earlier marriages to occur if premarital sex is common in the early years of courtship—yet only one marriage in this century involved a girl under twenty years of age. Also making for a strong case in favor of celibacy is the relatively high mean number of births per married women, averaging over five for the first half of this century (see Table 2). If we can assume from this a relatively high fecundity for the population, then the number of premarital conceptions should give us an accurate gauge of the degree of celibacy, or lack thereof. In fact, while premarital conceptions and illegitimate births did occur, they were the exception rather than the rule. There have been four children born of unmarried mothers in Kippel in this century. In addition, by calculating the time between marriage and the birth of the first child, we have found that in one out of 7.5 marriages, or slightly less than 14%, the first child was born less than eight months after the marriage. In other words, a relatively high proportion of all women were not pregnant prior to marriage, which at least hints at a high rate of celibacy, and it is likely that a similar rate prevailed among those who never married. This fact is im-

Table 2

Number of Children per Married Woman by Decade, 1900-1959 (Kippel)

Decade of Marriage	Average number of children (completed families, mother > age 45)	
	Mean	Standard Deviation
1900-09	6.9 ±4.4	
1910-19	4.9 ± 2.4	
1920-29	5.6 ± 3.6	
1930-39	5.1 ± 2.5	
1940-49	5.9 ± 4.0	
1950-59	4.6 ± 2.0	

portant in discussing fertility, for it can be assumed that late marriage and a large number of unmarried individuals in the population affect fertility and regulate population size only if these characteristics can be equated with celibacy. The combination of these factors—lack of birth control, late marriage, high fertility, small number of premarital conceptions, and low rate of illegitimacy—lends support to that assumption.

The actual number of nonreproducing individuals in the population is difficult to reconstruct for earlier periods in the valley history, due to the incomplete nature of the census data. However, based upon the author's census for 1970, there were 45 single residents over forty years of age, 17 between thirty and forty years old, and another 17 over twenty-five, for a total of 79 single individuals above the age of twenty-five. This figure is 34.5% of the 229 villagers over the age of 25. Considering celibacy in terms of the population over forty years of age, 45 of the 154 individuals in Kippel over forty in 1970, or 29.2%, never married, and are assumed to have no offspring.

Marriage and Potential Mates in Prewar Kippel

Despite the high rate of celibacy and late age of marriage, the population of Kippel grew from 248 in 1900 to 363 in 1950, an increase of 46%. Part of this increase was due to a marked reduction in infant mortality, with the rate declining from 247 per thousand births in the first decade of this century to 41 per thousand births in the decade 1960-69 (Friedl 1971:169). However, the growth in population size also indicates that fertility was high for married women, as seen in Table 2. Not only was the average number of children per married woman high, but the span between first and last child was relatively long, despite the late age of marriage for women (see Table 5 below).

During the traditional era of the valley's history, the selection of a potential mate was limited, and this is reflected in a high degree of inbreeding (see Friedl and Ellis 1974). Of 152 valley-endogamous marriages between 1900 and 1969, 67 were within the degree of relationship of third cousin. Prior to the Second World War, the economy and the ecological situation combined to enforce a strong pattern of endogamy. Economically, it was necessary to marry someone from the valley, preferably from one's own village or a neighboring village, in order to pool the inheritance of both spouses and create a viable agricultural unit sufficient to support a family. Ecologically, the severe physical barrier created by the mountains surrounding the valley on all four sides kept contact with the outside world to a minimum, creating both physical and cultural isolation. The combination of a strong tradition of agro-pastoral activity in the valley, and the tightness of community organization and allegiance to the family and church, imposed restrictions upon valley residents to remain at home and marry one of their own.

Postwar Economic and Demographic Change

In the years since World War II Kippel has undergone dramatic change, as indicated by the figures in Table 3 describing the occupational structure of the village. One result of the economic transformation of the village and the valley has been an increase in emigration, bringing with it a tendency toward valley-exogamous marriage and therefore a larger selection of potential mates. Since 1950 the emigration rate per decade has climbed from the prewar level of around 4% of the village population to over 9%. Along with this change has come an increase in the rate of

Table 3

Percent of Males Employed, by Occupation (Kippel)

Census year	Agriculture	Industry	Services
1941	76.3	4.4	19.3
1950	70.8	9.7	19.5
1960	36.4	41.7	21.9
1970	14.2	31.6	54.2

Table 4

Relationship between Age at Marriage and Employment in Kippel, 1940-1969

| | Average Age at Marriage | | Number of | Number of |
| | Males | Females | Males in Agriculture | Males in Industry |
Decade				
1940-49	30.3	29.1	82	6
1950-59	30.1	27.7	57	21
1960-69	27.2	26.0	26	43

r (1-2) = 0.92   r (1-3) = −0.93

exogamous marriage from a pre-1950 level of not quite 25% to a post-1950 rate of over 44%.

A number of other demographic changes have accompanied the decline in agriculture and the increased reliance upon industry and tourism. For one, growing economic independence of young people through nonagricultural employment has diminished the need to rely upon parental consent for use rights to the land in order to support a family. As a result, young men and women are no longer constrained by economic factors to delay marriage, and the average age at marriage has declined for both men and women, as indicated in Table 1 above. The decline in age at marriage after the Second World War is correlated strongly with the shift of males from agriculture to industry. These results are shown in Table 4.

Earlier marriage has not, however, resulted in a rise in the number of children. Rather, the number of children per married woman has declined from an average of over six for the first quarter of this century to 4.6 for the decade 1950-59.[5] Moreover, we might expect that the span from first to last child would have increased, but instead, it decreased from an average for the first five decades of the century of 9.6 years to 8.2 years for women completing their family in the decade 1950-59 (see Table 5).

Van de Walle has discussed strategies of family formation, in which late marriage gives way to early marriage as fertility comes under greater control. He points to two theories: one, presented by economic historians, is that population growth in eighteenth-century Europe "may have been

[5]Figures for the decade 1960-69 cannot be computed, since many families are not complete.

due not to mortality decline, but to a decline in the age at marriage and to the resulting increase in number of births." The second theory hold that "recent declines in age at marriage were made possible by the substitution of contraception for late marriage as the means of curbing population growth" (1972:141-2).

However, as van de Walle notes (1972:150), the perception of a causal relationship between decline in age at marriage and introduction of contraceptive practices is incorrect:

the existence of restrictions to early and general marriage and the use of contraception are essentially different in intent; the one is no substitute for the other. As a rule, contraception is practised efficiently by couples at a rather late stage in married life, after the desired family size has been reached.

In the case of Kippel, the data indicate a correlation between the decline in age at marriage and a smaller number of births per married woman. However, it is important to stress that the data do not indicate cause and effect. There is no reason to assume that decline in family size and the apparent use of contraception to achieve it were a prerequisite to reduction in age at marriage. Rather, we must assume that economic and social factors which led to the possibility of earlier marriage at the same time led to a desire to limit family size, while providing the means to achieve that end. Van de Walle suggests that had family size continued to increase as a result

Table 5

Mean Age at First and Last Child for Males and Females in Kippel, 1900-1969

Decade	Males			Females		
	Mean Age at First Child	Mean Age at Last Child	Mean Span	Mean Age at First Child	Mean Age at Last Child	Mean Span
1900-09	34.4	44.5	(10.1)	28.5	39.6	(11.1)
1910-19	32.4	43.2	(10.8)	29.4	41.8	(12.4)
1920-29	31.1	39.6	(8.5)	32.8	38.6	(5.8)
1930-39	32.8	42.4	(9.6)	30.7	40.2	(9.5)
1940-49	31.7	43.1	(11.4)	29.7	39.8	(10.1)
1950-59	33.4	39.6	(6.2)	29.4	37.6	(8.2)
1960-69	28.2	—	—	27.2	—	—

of earlier marriage, the general improvement in standard of living brought about by the economic transformation of the postwar era would have been negated. Such a conclusion seems to be more in accord with the data from Kippel.

Finally, Hajnal suggests that the pattern of high rate of celibacy found in western Europe (in 1900, 13% of men, 16% of women over 45 years of age; Hajnal 1965:102) has been disappearing since the Second World War. In Kippel, however, this does not appear to be the case, as indicated by the figures for 1970 in which 29.2% of the residents over the age of 40 had never married. Several reasons can be suggested to account for this apparent deviation from the general trend. First, there is the problem of culture lag. Modernization and the economic transformation of Kippel came relatively late, in the years following World War II; prior to that time, life in the Lötschental was much as it had always been, and little outside influence penetrated the valley economy and ideology. We might expect that in another generation, when the youth of today will be counted in the celibacy rate of those over 40, the rate will drop considerably.

Second, there is the religious tradition in the Lötschental which provides a basis for celibacy. Even today the secularization of the village has only just begun. There is still a strong tendency to avoid premarital sex, a general ignorance of sexual practices and birth control, especially among unmarried persons, and a great deal of apprehension among unmarried youths concerning sexual contact. Courting patterns, while slightly more modern and in keeping with the changing times, still emphasize a long period of a steady relationship between two people with no expectation of premarital sex. Thus although the economic conditions surrounding the pattern of inheritance and the dependence of the heir upon the parents have now changed so that they so longer inhibit marriage and promote celibacy, other social factors have stepped in to take their place.

Kippel is in a period of transition, and many traditions, among them reluctance to marry early or at all, are retained despite economic and social conditions which no longer promote them. As a result, the population size of the village, while rising, is still being held in check to some extent by customary behavior patterns. In the future we might expect that these traditions will disappear; yet at the same time, as the village becomes more secularized, we also expect to find a reduction of family size because of greater reliance upon artificial means of contraception. The question is whether a decline in the birth rate will accompany, or even precede, a growth in the rate of marriage. In other words, will the more effective artificial means of contraception replace the less effective practices of late marriage and celibacy rapidly enough to offset the increased proportion of married individuals in the population as celibacy and late marriage decline? We think it will not, and that the population of the village will continue in a period of rapid growth for at least another decade, until such time as economic conditions no longer hold the promise for a rising standard of living in a period of continued population growth. At such a time (which has already been experienced in many western countries), we expect to see the same kinds of changes in Kippel and other villages like it that we are witnessing today in western nations.

ACKNOWLEDGMENTS

This paper is based upon research conducted by Friedl in Kippel, Canton Valais, Switzerland in 1969-70 and 1972. Fieldwork from September 1969 through September 1970 was supported by the National Institutes of Health Grant GM-1224. Fieldwork during the summer of 1972 was carried out with the assistance of a Grant-in-Aid from the College of Social and Behavioral Sciences, The Ohio State University. The authors wish to thank Drs. Jana Hesser, Gabriel Lasker, William Petersen, and Etienne van de Walle, for their helpful comments and criticisms.

Received: 5 May 1975.

LITERATURE CITED

ARENSBERG, CONRAD M.   1937   The Irish countryman. (Reprinted 1968) The Natural History Press, Garden City, N.Y.

COLE, JOHN W.   1971   Estate and inheritance in the Italian Alps. Research Reports No. 10, Department of Anthropology, University of Massachusetts, Amherst.

FRIEDL, JOHN   1971   Economic and social change in a Swiss Alpine village. Unpublished Ph.D. Dissertation, Department of Anthropology, University of California, Berkeley.

———   1973a   Benefits of fragmentation in a traditional society: A case from the Swiss Alps. Human Organization **32**: 29-36.

———   1973b   Alternatives to division: Partible inheritance in the Swiss Alps. Journal of the Steward Anthropological Society **4**: 70-78.

———   1974   Kippel: A changing village in the Alps. Holt, Rinehart and Winston, New York.

FRIEDL, JOHN AND WALTER S. ELLIS   1974   Inbreeding, isonymy, and isolation in a Swiss communtiy. Human Biology **45**: 699-712.

HAJNAL, J.   1965   European marriage patterns in perspective. *In:* D. V. Glass and D. E. C. Eversley, eds., Population in history, pp. 101-143. Aldine, Chicago.

VAN DE WALLE, ETIENNE   1972   Marriage and marital fertility. *In:* Population and social change. D. V. Glass and R. Revelle, (eds.). Edward Arnold Ltd., London.

Adaptive Childbearing in a North Slope Eskimo Community[1]

By George S. Masnick[2] and Solomon H. Katz[3]

ABSTRACT

Examination of Eskimo data in 11 censuses from 1940 to 1970 of Barrow, Alaska, permitted identification of surviving births with their mothers. The fertility of women was traced through several periods of economic depression. Population pyramids, period fertility and cohort fertility were recorded. Women who began reproduction during periods of prosperity had high fertility and short birth intervals which persisted through periods of adversity. Those cohorts which met economic hardship when young had reduced fertility and longer birth intervals then and in subsequent periods of adversity. These findings are at variance with traditional demographic transition theory.

THE LEGACY OF DEMOGRAPHIC TRANSITION THEORY

Does there have to be social change on a large scale, of the kind we identify with the words "industrialization," "urbanization" and "economic development" before human beings will voluntarily and effectively control fertility? To those whose thinking on this question has been conditioned by Demographic Transition Theory, the answer tends toward the affirmative. According to this framework a pattern of below maximum fertility in more "traditional" societies is thought to be determined by over-arching biological and cultural forces beyond volition, such as sterility, mating patterns, breastfeeding practices, postpartum and menstrual taboos, fetal wastage, anovulatory cycles and the like. On the whole, however, levels of fertility in these societies would be expected to be very high, an adaptation to compensate for the high mortality chracteristic of such populations. Fertility would also be relatively inflexible, since the "intermediate variables" (Davis and Blake, 1956) of exposure to intercourse, conception, gestation and parturition were seen as themselves inflexible. Only after

[1]The authors would like to thank Joan Schall, Pam Gottesman, Fatimah Deffaa, Alan Sacks, Don Denny and Don Goldstein for their assistance in compiling and processing the data set on which this paper reports. Preliminary reports on this analysis were presented at the annual meeting of the American Anthropological Association, New Orleans (November 1973) and at the Third International Symposium on Circumpolar Health, Yellowknife, N.W.T. (July 1974).
[2]Department of Population Sciences, Harvard University, Cambridge, Mass.
[3]Department of Anthropology, University of Pennsylvania, Philadelphia, Pa.

"modernization" with the attendant social mobility, urban life styles, diminishing economic utility and increasing costs of children, the weighing of opportunity costs, contraceptive sophistication, and reproductive rationality would voluntary fertility regulation emerge.

It is not our intent in this paper to review the multifarious studies and reinterpretations of them which constitute nothing less than a full scale debate over the accuracy of Demographic Transition Theory. We are fortunate in having several timely reviews and critiques recently published which summarize many of the relevant themes (Coale, 1973; Teitelbaum, 1975). Suffice it to point out that Transition Theory has been under attack from several quarters, from historical demographers (Wrigley, 1966; van de Walle and Knodel, 1967; Demeny, 1968), from anthropologists, (other contributors in this issue; Dumond, 1975) and from the family planners (Bogue, 1969), who see their particular strategy as providing a ready solution to the high growth rates we are experiencing throughout most of the world today. At stake in this debate is whether we should view all peoples as possessing the capacity to regulate their fertility voluntarily, if and when it is in their best interest to do so. Is conscious fertility control a basic adaptive element woven into the cultural fabric of most societies throughout history as an aid to their survival? If this is so, then we must add this social dimension as one more selective force to our schemes for the interpretation of human evolution. Should we view high rates of natural increase in Third World populations today as a short run phase coming at a time when ongoing social change has temporarily undermined the traditional motivation and methods for fertility regulation, and where rapid early childbearing is not viewed as dysfunctional by young adults? Can we expect a balance to be restored between births and deaths without disastrous increases in mortality or massive intervention to prevent births? Finally, in light of these possibilities, how can we develop evolutionary models that can help us to interpret the current evolutionary status of various human populations throughout the world.

No sure answer can be given to the above questions until the passage of time reveals what the future course of events will be in what is termed by Western standards the "less developed" populations of the world. In the meantime, we can make qualified judgments from our knowledge of the demographic history of populations prior to, during, and subsequent to their undergoing social and demographic change. The problem we face is that the documentation of such historical events is sketchy at best, and for most populations outside of Western Europe and North America, the data are practically non-existent. Where the data do exist, it therefore becomes all the more important to undertake an analysis of these data in order to gain a better understanding of the demographic processes that determine the growth and structure of human populations.

To date, the most persuasive arguments in favor of voluntary fertility regulation in pre-industrial populations have come from studies of European agricultural populations in the Eighteenth and Nineteenth Centuries (Wrigley, 1966; Coale, 1969), and from African Bush populations whose sustenance is gained from hunting and gathering activities (Dumond, 1975). In the former case the evidence is largely the empirical demonstration that fertility rates for married women fall significantly below what would be expected in the absence of birth control, particularly in the later reproductive ages where the truncation of fertility rates is similar to the pattern revealed in modern populations where contraception is in widespread use to terminate childbearing after desired family size is achieved. Finally, the interval between the penultimate and final birth in these populations is substantially longer than prior birth intervals. Couples practicing birth control during this part of their reproductive ages will contribute a longer last interbirth interval if the final birth is either accidental, the result of a desire to replace children that have died subsequent to the decision to stop, or a simple change of heart about wanting an additional child.

For hunters and gatherers, the inference about deliberate fertility control is somewhat more conjectural. The long interbirth intervals found at all parities is explained as the result of a conscious desire to space children far enough apart so the mother's geographic mobility, necessary for survival, would not be hampered by the need to carry two infants. The moderate levels of fertility that would result under such a regime of birthspacing would be sufficient to maintain the population only under stable ecological conditions. In periods following sudden increases in mortality, or following migration into a new territory, much higher levels of fertility would be necessary to restore the population to a critical and viable size. Once the niche is filled, however, and resources begin to thin, necessitating greater mobility, the lower fertility levels once again become important. The reasoning is that only if volition plays an important role can the requisite birth spacing and rapid readjustments in fertility levels be guaranteed.

The present debate about voluntary fertility regulation in preindustrial populations can be summarized in two questions. Can we say that it has been conclusively demonstrated that fertility is sensitive to changing social and economic conditions in pre-modern populations? And, can we safely say that apparent fluctuations and trends in fertility in preindustrial societies is volitional in nature and not produced primarily by shifts in the probability of conception, fetal wastage and infant mortality? The latter question is particularly voiced by those who hypothesize that effective fertility levels are very much tied to nutrition, which is expected to change significantly as social and economic conditions change (Frisch, 1975). Given the difficulty in uncovering trends and variations in conceptions, miscarriages, stillbirths and infant deaths in the kinds of data available for these populations, such questions are bound to remain with us for a long time to come. We shall deal further with these competing hypotheses, nutritional vs. volitional, in our discussion below.

THE POPULATION OF BARROW, ALASKA

What is needed at this juncture are additional studies of fertility change drawn from a wider range of societies, particularly those without a tradition of late marriage age and low proportion married characteristic of European societies, and those less isolated from the forces of modernization than the hunters and gatherers of the African bush. The community of Barrow, located on the northern most point of the north slope of Alaska, and the community nearest to Prudhoe Bay, provides just such an opportunity for study. Over the last 50 years, Barrow has grown from a small distant outpost of mostly Eskimo families banded together as hunters in a life style inherited from generations past, to become a town of over 2000 with a movie house, several stores, a bank, a hospital, a large public school and much more. The rapidity of Barrow's transformation into a 20th century town has meant that traditional norms and values influencing patterns of fertility under earlier conditions were very much present as social change swept over the community. Furthermore, although Barrow's transition has been repaid, it has not been smooth. Quickly alternating periods of depression and prosperity can provide a stimulus to test the sensitivity of fertility to changing circumstances.

From the introduction of a cash economy with reindeer herding in the beginning of this century to the current activities surrounding the development of the North Slope oil fields, the sweeping economic changes can best be described as "boom or bust". The reindeer industry in Barrow started collapsing during the mid 1920's when the price per carcass dropped from $5.00 to $2.00. The reindeer economy was succeeded by a lively trade in Artic fox fur, but when pelts selling from $50.00-$100.00 apiece in 1929 declined to $5.00 in 1932, the only sources of cash in the village disappeared until World War II. During the war the active exploration for oil reserves brought a huge boom in employment until about 1952 when the initial exploration was completed, whereupon another period of economic depression followed. By 1958 another boom atmosphere was begun with the construction of the "Dew Line" early warning defensive radar sites and the location of the Naval Arctic Research Laboratories. Throughout the 1960's the economy remained relatively stable with employment related first to various Federal and State projects and then more recently to the Alaska pipeline gradually replacing those activities earlier tied to the Cold War. Finally, the Native Land Claim Settlement signed into law in 1971, which provided Alaska Eskimos and Indians 40 million acres of land, a $462.5 million cash settlement and $500 million in mineral rights on lands no longer owned by the natives, will insure that economic and social change will continue at a rapid pace in the near future (Katz, 1972).

Not only does the natural isolation and profound social changes make Barrow a significant community in relation to the questions raised above, but we are fortunate in having much of the demographic change documented in a series of eleven censuses of this population conducted between 1940 and 1970. The years in which a census was taken are 1940, 1944, 1946, 1950, 1951, 1954, 1957, 1958, 1962, 1966 and 1970. Figure 1

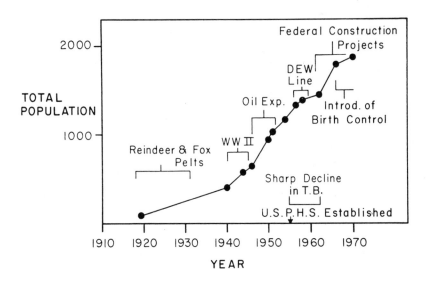

FIG. 1.　Population Growth of Barrow Alaska

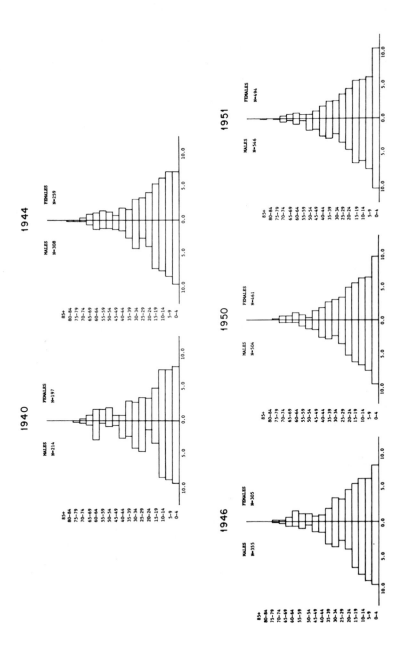

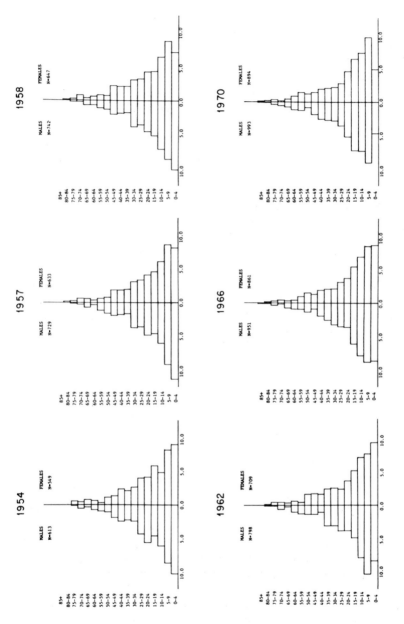

FIG 2. Barrow Age Structures 1940-1970

indicates the scope of social and demographic change over the 30 year period covered by the censuses.

The censuses collected information on date and place of birth, identity of natural parents, and other information useful in establishing a record linkage of individuals through the censuses. Families could be reconstituted from the longitudinal file that was established, and births derived by noting additions to families between consecutive censuses. The census data were supplemented by a geneology of Barrow families compiled in the late 1960's, and from partial vital statistics data. While the study of fertility using census counts tends to underestimate the total level of childbearing due to the omission of children who are born and die between censuses, this bias operates equally in the case where families are reconstituted from civil or parish registers, where infants who die shortly after birth frequently go unrecorded. This problem exists to an even greater extent when the Child Women Ratio (CWR), or the number of children age 0-4 per 1000 women age 15-49 as recorded in the census is the fertility measure (Robinson, 1963). With the CWR, infant deaths in the first five years are subject to being unreported, whereas the intercensal interval in the Barrow data ranges from only one to four years. Recognizing the confounding effects of trends and fluctuations in infant and early childhood mortality, however, we will place an emphasis on a type cohort analysis that attempts to deal with this problem.

AGE STRUCTURES AND GROWTH RATES

From our understanding of the manner in which the age structure of a population is determined we can roughly gauge the changing pattern of vital rates by simple inspection of the changes in age structure (Coale, 1957). Figure 2 presents the age/sex structures of the Barrow population for the eleven census dates. In the first several censuses, the uneven population pyramid that broadens gradually at the base is characteristic of a small population where fertility is moderately high, but where simple stochastic fluctuations in births, deaths and migration typical in small populations would result in a lumpy age distribution. By the early 1950's the population has grown and vital events stabilized sufficiently to produce a smoother age structure. The primary source of unevenness during this period is the expanding cohort of births being introduced at the base of the pyramid. Such a pattern indicates a period of rising fertility. By the late 1950's and throughout the 1960's, the gradual blunting of the base, most notable in 1966, is indicative of a period of declining birth rates. By 1970 a sharp drop in fertility is evident.

Table 1

Rates of Population Growth in Barrow, 1940-1970

Period	Population at beginning of period	Population at end of period	Average annual exponential period rate of growth
1940-44	411	567	8.0%
1944-46	567	660	7.6
1946-50	660	965	9.5
1950-51	965	1040	7.5
1951-54	1040	1162	3.7
1954-57	1162	1362	5.3
1957-58	1362	1389	2.0
1958-62	1389	1507	2.0
1962-66	1507	1812	4.6
1966-70	1812	1887	1.0

In addition to changing age structures, the population of Barrow has grown significantly in size over the thirty year period under study. Table 1 presents the rates of growth over each intercensal period. Migration has obviously played an important role in the growth of Barrow in the early years. We know that, at most, a population can grow by about four percent a year due to an excess of births over deaths, when a high Crude Birth Rate is around 50 and a low Crude Death Rate near 10 per 1000. Having growth rates between 7.5 and 9.5 percent in the 1940-50 decade, a substantial amount of inmigration must have occurred during this period. The low growth rates in the 1960's probably indicate that the migration pattern has become reversed, with more people moving out than in.

Such a preliminary scan of age structures and rates of growth affords some insight into the demographic forces operating in a population, but because these population parameters involve the net outcome of fertility, mortality and migration acting simultaneously, it is difficult to assign independent weight to any of these factors with accuracy unless a further decomposition and analysis of the data is undertaken. We shall proceed with such an analysis of childbearing patterns, first focusing on period age specific fertility rates, then cohort rates and finally on cohort patterns of birthspacing.

PERIOD FERTILITY

Period age specific fertility rates were constructed in the following manner. For each census, women were grouped into five year age groups,

Table 2

Average Age Specific Period Fertility Rates While in Barrow

Age at beginning of period	1940-44	1944-46	1946-50	1950-51	Intercensal Period					
					1951-54	1954-57	1957-58	1958-62	1962-66	1966-70
15-19	0.13	0.12	0.18	0.08	0.15	0.14	0.19	0.25	0.20	0.06
20-24	0.30	0.38	0.35	0.35	0.34	0.31	0.31	0.41	0.33	0.17
25-29	0.31	0.38	0.37	0.41	0.39	0.39	0.30	0.48	0.22	0.10
30-34	0.46	0.33	0.28	0.26	0.21	0.25	0.24	0.45	0.33	0.04
35-39	0.30	0.12	0.07	0.23	0.20	0.21	0.15	0.19	0.04	0.05
40-44	*	0.23	*	0.31	0.15	0.12	0.07	0.09	0.11	0.13
TFR†	7.50	7.80	6.25	8.20	7.20	7.10	6.30	9.35	6.15	2.75

*Based on less than 10 women (see Appendix for population sizes).

†The TFR, or Total Fertility Rate, is derived by assuming that a hypothetical woman would experience the given age specific fertility rate for five years before moving into the next age group, where her fertility would again be five times the yearly rate, and so on until fertility is cumulated until the end of the last age group.

15-19, 20-24, 25-29, etc. The number of their children recorded in that census, or any previous census, were listed, and the average cumulative fertility for women in each age group was computed. For the early census the older children of women in their late 40's have a greater chance of having moved out of Barrow, thus biasing cumulative fertility for women at these ages downward. This problem would not exist in the later censuses, since once a child was linked at birth with a mother in an earlier census, he or she figured in the cumulative fertility of the mother at all subsequent censuses. For consistency, however, we use the age group 40-44 to mark the end of the reproductive period. The interval between two consecutive censuses is the base period over which childbearing was then examined. For example, women age 15-19 in 1940 would be age 19-23 in 1944, and the cumulative fertility of this latter group, when compared with the former, would indicate the extent of childbearing over the period. Dividing through by the number of years in the period would produce average annual age specific fertility rates. These figures are recorded in Table 2. Bearing in mind that the measure of fertility thus produced underestimates the level, perhaps by as much as 10-20%, but undoubtedly reflects both the overall age pattern and the temporal swings quite accurately, the following features of Table 2 should be noted.

Childbearing in the age group 15-19 is very low throughout most of the thirty year period, by comparison to levels in the next two age groups, and by comparison to levels in other modern populations that fall into the "pre-industrial" category. If ethnographic reports of widespread teenage sexual activity among Eskimos are correct, this relatively slow start at childbearing demands close attention in future studies.

The 20-24 year age group begins to demonstrate the temporal swing in fertility that is a dominant pattern in this population. Those in the 20-24 age group in 1940 were having children at the rate of about 1.5 births over the five year period. Adjusting for infant mortality, this would be about one birth every three years, which is significantly lower than the rate of childbearing that would be expected in a Malthusian population where birth intervals average closer to two years. The reduced level of fertility that is observed could either be the outcome of factors insuring a diffused pattern of adequate spacing for a hunting society, or a temporary response to the Depression and early years of World War II. In the immediate post-War period fertility in this age group rose and then gradually tapered off until the 1958-62 period when there was a sharp rise. Finally, we observe a sharp decline in the last two periods 1962-66 and 1966-70.

The pattern of fertility for the 25-29 age group parallels that of the younger age group with one important difference. There is no evidence of a decline in the post-War upsurge until the late 1950's. It appears that women who accelerated their childbearing during the immediate post-War period when they were in their early 20's continued the high pace of childbearing in their late 20's, which occurred during a period of gradually intensifying economic depression in Barrow between 1952 and 1958. We shall have more to say about this pattern below.

The age group 30-34 again repeats the pattern of declining fertility followed by a strong spurt in 1958-62, and a sharp decline afterwards. This age group showed the largest swing in fertility of any age group. Women who began their reproductive period under conditions of stress during the late 1930's and early 1940's appeared able to control childbearing during the 1950's recession, whereas by contrast those who began childbearing during the period of post-War prosperity, and reached age 30-34 during the 1958-62 boom had exceptionally high fertility. Looking at the childbearing patterns in this manner is to adopt a cohort approach, and we shall develop this line of analysis further in the next section.

Interpretation of the period rates for age groups 35-39 and 40-44 confounds the effects of stochastic fluctuation due to decreasing population size, cohort vs. period effects and sharply diminishing age specific fertility. Therefore, little can be introduced by way of clarification for the pattern we observe in these age groups unless we shift to a cohort analysis.

Another reason that the period rates are not the best fertility measures to focus upon is the arbitrary way in which the intercensal intervals cut across both periods of prosperity and depression. Finally, the figures in Table 2 refer to women who are in a given age group in the *beginning* of the intercensal period. Since the typical woman would spend part of the period exposed at the rate in the subsequent age group, the period fertility rates can give a distorted impression of the pattern of childbearing, especially when there are abrupt changes in the rates in contiguous age groups. We have presented the period rates in spite of these shortcomings since they are the most straightforward to produce, are usually the only rates that can be computed for many populations without a longitudinal record, and they do reveal the nature of the fertility pattern for the younger age groups before the confounding of cohort with period effects.

COHORT FERTILITY

The principle behind cohort fertility analysis is described well in the following quotation from Kiser, et al. (1958 p. 255).

> We may think of the cohort approach as an attempt to study the continuing *process* of changing fertility rates as they are observed throughout the reproductive period,

rather than to compare points within the process as if they were isolated from each other. Cohort analysis proceeds on the assumption that rates at various stages of the reproductive period are not isolated in reality, but strongly influence one another. What happens early in the process affects what happens later.

Cohort fertility rates of Barrow women are found in Table 3. Also given are the dates the cohorts entered the particular age groups as an aid in the analysis. The rates represent the actual childbearing of birth cohorts as they pass through the reproductive ages, and the table should be read across by following a particular cohort through the childbearing years. The difference that one observes between cohorts by reading down the columns can be attributed to that fact that each cohort had a prior history of childbearing and were bearing their children at given ages in different time periods.

The swing in total completed fertility observed in the period data is revealed also in the cohort rates, with some important patterns revealed in the age specific breakdowns. The initial downward trend extended through the cohorts born from 1915-19. Even though a major part of their reproductive ages came after World War II, when conditions were more favorable to childbearing, fertility was not "made up" by this group who got off to a slow start at childbearing. They seemed to be unusually responsive in lowering their fertility in response to the recessions of the early 1940's and late 1950's (while they were age 25-29 and 40-44), and all told, their completed fertility was reduced.

The rapid early childbearing of the post World War II period resulted in a baby boom for the 1925-29 cohort. As time passed, this cohort showed a low capacity for controlling their later fertility during the 1955-59 and 1965-69 periods (when they entered the 30-34 and 40-44 age groups). Their level of recession childbearing might well be attributed to their lack of an early experience in controlling fertility. It is hypothesized that the 1925-29 birth cohort of Barrow mothers shared the motivation to control fertility during the later recessions. Indeed, since they already had larger family sizes at these dates they would be perhaps more motivated to control their births. But, in contrast to the 1915-19 cohort, these women were unable to invoke the behavior necessary to do so.

The decline in age-specific fertility of all cohorts has been especially dramatic in the years 1965-69 for all cohorts except those born 1925-29. Even the 1930-34 cohort, who began childbearing at an extremely fast pace, controlled their fertility dramatically as they entered the age group 35-39. This pattern suggests that the modern contraceptive technology introduced to this population by the Public Health Service in the late 1960's, can reduce fertility in a cohort that might ordinarily not be expected to use the traditional fertility regulating mechanisms effectively. The

Table 3

Cohort Childbearing While in Barrow. Number of Births per Woman During Five Year Age Intervals for Women Born Between 1900 and 1949.†

Age Specific	Fertility and Date Cohort Entered Age Group (in parentheses)						Cumulative
Cohort Born Total in Years Age 44	15-19	20-24	25-29	30-34	35-39	40-44	Through
1900-04	*	*	*	*	*	2.01 (1940-44)	8.46
1905-09	*	*	*	*	2.32 (1940-44)	0.89 (1945-49)	7.41
1910-14	*	*	*	1.97 (1940-44)	1.11 (1945-49)	1.44 (1950-54)	6.52
1915-19	*	*	1.50 (1940-45)	1.56 (1945-49)	1.54 (1950-54)	0.12 (1955-59)	5.93

1920-24	*	0.91 (1940-44)	1.52 (1945-49)	2.18 (1950-54)	1.33 (1955-59)	0.51 (1960-64)	6.44
1925-29	0.07 (1940-44)	1.05 (1945-49)	1.68 (1950-54)	1.66 (1955-59)	1.86 (1960-64)	0.48 (1965-69)	6.80
1930-34	0.10 (1945-49)	0.88 (1950-54)	1.66 (1955-59)	2.36 (1960-64)	0.55 (1965-69)	*	*
1935-39	0.17 (1950-54)	1.02 (1955-59)	1.92 (1960-64)	1.31 (1965-69)	*	*	*
1940-44	0.18 (1955-59)	1.32 (1960-64)	1.16 (1965-69)	*	*	*	*
1945-49	0.12 (1960-64)	0.67 (1965-69)	*	*	*	*	*

†Figures are net of children born and dying in the intercensal interval.
*Indicates childbearing period is outside the 1940-1970 census range.

1930-34 birth cohort was still young enough in 1965-69 to adopt the innovation in contraceptive technology, but because of fifteen prior years of regular pregnancy and childbearing, probably would have been too old to control fertility effectively by traditional methods requiring sustained motivation and a disruption of patterned sexual and childbearing behavior.

To sum up, those cohorts who entered the childbearing ages during bad times got off to a slower than expected start at family formation, and also demonstrated a better ability to adjust their fertility later in the reproductive period when the next depression struck the community. This pattern of childbearing is contrasted with that of other cohorts who began reproduction under conditions of relative prosperity and rapid early fertility, and who later showed less of an ability to adjust their pace of childbearing downward during depression years. These findings are significant in that they lead us away from traditional demographic transition theory which argues that the Malthusian checks of delayed marriage and higher infant mortality have primarily operated to control pre-industrial population growth, with birth control a feature having evolved only in modern urban-industrial populations. Instead, our initial results are suggestive of a theory in which childbearing is more sensitive to individual prerogative, regardless of the general level of economic development of a community. Our interpretation of the pattern of age-specific fertility rates has led us to hypothesize that lack of individual motivation to regulate births during the younger reproductive ages results in a "trained incapacity" to regulate births later, even in the face of circumstances where additional childbearing means hardship for family and community. Contrariwise, the learning experience gained by those cohorts who lowered their rates of fertility early in the childbearing period, however modestly, was necessary to reinforce behavioral and attiudinal sets relating to the effective practice of birth control in later years.

In the following section we shall address further the question of temporal swings in fertility in this population by examining trends and differentials in cohort patterns of birth spacing. By focusing upon birth intervals we are better able to isolate the influence of ongoing changes in social and economic conditions and distinguish the impact of these changes for women with different patterns of previous childbearing.

THE PATTERN OF BIRTH INTERVALS

Following the lead of others who have addressed the questions of fertility regulation in pre-industrial populations, most notably Henry

(1956) and Wrigley (1966) we shall examine the pattern of early childbearing by analysis of the interval between first and second and between second and third births. With this focus we will be able to demonstrate whether the fluctuations in fertility rates in early childbearing ages identified in the previous section are due simply to delays in marriage and the onset of childbearing, or to variations in spacing once childbearing has been begun. If our interpretation of the cohort fertility rates in terms of stressing an acquired ability by delaying fertility while young is correct, we should be able to demonstrate swings in early birth intervals when mothers are young. Also, if incentives for fertility control operate partly in connection with the number of children already born, or at a time when a couple desires to stop further childbearing altogether, the interval between the penultimate and last birth should be revealing.

Table 4 presents the trend in birth spacing for the first few births while the women were towards the beginning of their reproductive periods. By restricting the focus to women in ages 20-29, we have attempted to identify what was occurring when the timing of childbearing behavior was at or near the census date. As can be seen in the first column, the pattern proceeds from relatively long intervals between first and second birth, on the order

Table 4

Mean Birth Intervals (Months) of Women Ages 20-29 at Census Date for First to Second and Second to Third Births

Census Date	Mean Birth Interval Women Age 20-29 at Census Date			
	1-2 Births		2-3 Births	
1940	34.2	(35)*	38.5	(24)
1944	35.8	(36)	35.3	(27)
1946	33.4	(34)	34.2	(22)
1950	22.8	(47)	21.5	(35)
1951	20.6	(47)	21.9	(33)
1954	21.3	(55)	21.2	(39)
1957	24.9	(53)	19.1	(44)
1958	27.7	(56)	19.4	(42)
1962	24.7	(65)	18.3	(48)
1966	21.1	(78)	17.2	(52)
1970	20.2	(67)	20.6	(41)

*Number in parentheses is number of women on which mean was computed.

of almost three years, for childbearing before the end of World War II,
followed by a sharp decrease in the delay to the second child after the War,
with a gradual rise until 1958 when, again, a pattern of shorter spacing
emerged. This swing in the length of the first inter-birth interval is parallel
to the trend we observed in our earlier analysis of age-specific period
fertility rates.

The second column of Table 4 examines the pattern in spacing between
the second and third births. The secular decline in average length of the
birth interval continues uninterrupted, with the depression of the 1950's
seemingly having no effect on the spacing. However, if what we have
argued about the impact of rapid early childbearing on later fertility is true,
we would expect that women who had their first and second children
quickly would be less likely to be able to adjust their fertility to changing
circumstances. Thus, women still in their twenties and having their third
child during the recession years 1952-1958, were those who had their first
two children during the post-war prosperity years, and would have been
least likely to have acquired an ability to control fertility during that period.

Another way of examining whether deliberate birth control is influencing the level of childbearing is by focusing upon the interval between
the last two children and contrasting this figure with the mean birth
interval for all previous births. These figures are presented in Table 5 along
with age and mean number of children in 1970 for different birth cohorts of
mothers. Women born 1900-1909 began their childbearing before Bar-

Table 5

*Difference Between Last and Previous Birth Intervals For Various Cohorts
of Barrow Women*

(1)	(2)	(3)	(4)	(5)	(6)	(7)
Year of Birth of Mother	Size of Sample	Mean Last Birth Interval	Mean all Previous Birth Intervals	Difference (3) - (4)	Central Age in 1970	Mean Number Children in 1970*
1900-09	32	36.9	38.2	−1.3	65	7.81
1910-19	46	38.7	33.6	5.1	55	7.47
1920-29	65	29.9	24.3	5.6	45	7.81
1930-39	64	29.5	24.1	5.4	35	6.01
1940-49	38	22.2	17.6	4.6	25	4.21

*Mean number of children for those women in the cohort having three or more children.

row's economy began to shift toward "modern." Their long intervals are consistent with traditional Eskimo social structures where natural factors, such as prolonged breast feeding, operate to regulate fertility. It is not surprising, therefore, that there are no differences between last and prior intervals in this cohort. For succeeding cohorts of mothers a clear distinction between last birth interval and previous intervals, on the order of five months, has emerged. The hypothesis is that deliberate fertility regulation will show up in a pronounced effect on the last birth interval. An alternative hypothesis that last birth intervals, coming late in the reproductive period as they do, and are influenced by declining fecundity or increased fetal wastage as a result of aging of the cohort, fails to account for the persistence of the pattern for the two younger cohorts who are still in their prime childbearing years in 1970. Another pattern revealed in Table 5 supportive of the idea that birth control was practiced by this population is contained in the last column. In the cohort of 1920-29, those women having three or more children had an average family size of 7.81, the same as women born 20 years previously. The spacing of the later cohort, however, was shorter on the average of about one year between births. This meant that they would finish childbearing, on the average, seven or eight years earlier, providing that childbearing started about the same age in both cohorts. In any case, shorter birth intervals must be accompanied by a more efficient practice of birth control at one end or the other of the reproductive period if family size is not to increase.

CONCLUDING REMARKS

Our examination of birth interval data for Barrow women lends additional support to the interpretation that Eskimo populations have in the past been able rapidly to adjust fertility to changes in social and economic conditions. Those cohorts who began childbearing under adversity demonstrated an early ability to space their births. Those whose first two children came quickly at the beginning of the reproductive ages were less able to slow the birth of their third child, even though social and economic circumstances would warrant a delay. As would be expected in a population practicing deliberate birth control, all cohorts had differentials between the last and previous birth intervals during this period of rapid social change. In this sense, our paper presents dramatic evidence that the requisite knowledge of fertility regulation is to be found in native populations not previously exposed to "modern" concepts of contraception and family planning. It suggests that more focused studies of other small native populations might lead to a broader theory of the relations between individual fertility control and non-Western social conditions.

For Eskimos, the traditional explanation of fertility regulation through infanticide is not a satisfactory one, since cohorts with rapid early childbearing would be the most likely to adopt this method having both the problems and the security deriving from their living children to justify such extreme measures. Likewise, the hypothesis that fluctuating nutritional levels might account for the fertility swing does not account for the particular cohort patterns we observe. Those expected to experience the greatest nutritional deprivation are women with a history of high fertility, who have larger family sizes and are more likely to have small children. Instead, these mothers showed the least sensitivity to adjusting the pace of childbearing. Rather, the data suggest we should be looking for birth control practices that require a learning period to be used effectively. These include the gamut of traditional techniques such as periodic abstinence, withdrawal, abortion, breastfeeding and other possible folk methods. Should other populations in less modern societies be found to be receptive to such techniques, our findings suggest that local family planning programs should present these "natural" alternatives to cohorts in the early stages of their reproductive periods, before rapid early childbearing results in a learned incapacity to use such methods effectively. The present strategy of many programs, to concentrate on older women who have rapidly achieved their desired family size, will find little success with traditional methods. Such programs rely upon the modern technologies of pill and IUD, but these too require sustained motivation to use effectively. Once our knowledge of the circumstances that motivate traditional populations to regulate fertility is improved, and the techniques of birth control used by such peoples better understood, we may be able to correct the failures present in existing programs attempting to help people regulate their fertility in modernizing populations throughout the world.

Received: 2 September 1975

LITERATURE CITED

BOGUE, D. J.   1969   Principles of demography. Wiley, New York, pp. 656-658.

COALE, A. J.   1957   How the age distribution of a human population is determined. Cold Spring Harbor Symposia on Quantitative Biology, 22: 83-89.

————   1969   The decline of fertility in Europe from the French Revolution to World War II. *In:* S. J. Behrman, et al., (eds.) Fertility and family planning: A world view. University of Michigan Press, Ann Arbor, pp. 3-24.

————   1973   The demographic transition. International Union for the Scientific Study of Population, Liège, pp. 53-71.

DAVIS, K. AND J. BLAKE   1956   Social structure and fertility: an analytic framework. Economic Development and Cultural Change, 4: 211-235.

DEMENY, P. 1968 Early fertility decline in Austria-Hungary: a lesson in demographic transition. Daedalus, **974:** 502-522.

DUMOND, D. E. 1975 The limitation of human population: a natural history. Science, **187:** 713-721.

FRISCH, R. 1975 Demographic implications of the biological determinants of female fecundity. Social Biology, **22:** 17-22.

HENRY, L. 1956 Anciennes familles genevoises. Institut national d'études démographiques, Paris, pp. 93-110.

KATZ, S. 1972 Change on top of the world. Expeditions, **15:** 15-21.

KISER, C. V. et al. 1968 Trends and variations in fertility in the United States. Harvard University Press, Cambridge.

TEITELBAUM 1975 Relevance of demographic transition theory for developing countries. Science, **188:** 420-425.

VAN DE WALLE, E. AND J. KNODEL 1967 Demographic transition and fertility decline, the European case. International Union for the Scientific Study of Population, Sydney, pp. 47-55.

WRIGLEY, E. A. 1966 Family limitation in pre-industrial England. Economic History Review, **19:** 82-109.

Appendix A

Male Population of Barrow, Alaska at Eleven Census Dates

Age Group	Population at Census Date										
	1940	1944	1946	1950	1951	1954	1957	1958	1962	1966	1970
0-4	39	54	62	92	109	119	156	142	125	157	90
5-9	36	48	58	73	78	101	126	120	155	159	172
10-14	35	43	52	65	66	71	83	100	119	143	139
15-19	14	41	45	61	69	54	64	72	74	112	138
20-24	6	22	27	51	48	65	66	64	58	67	98
25-29	19	15	19	34	37	51	50	50	58	64	68
30-34	17	24	25	23	24	29	51	53	46	59	55
35-39	10	15	22	32	31	27	23	25	46	46	53
40-44	11	9	11	25	27	29	24	26	17	36	48
45-49	3	8	10	14	16	23	27	29	22	17	34
50-54	4	7	4	13	17	12	22	19	22	26	16
55-59	2	7	7	9	4	11	16	16	21	18	24
60-64	12	8	5	4	9	9	5	10	17	18	23
65-69	3	4	5	4	4	5	10	10	4	14	14
70-74	2	1	2	4	5	6	4	3	10	3	10
75-79	1	1	1	0	1	1	2	3	2	8	7
80-84	0	1	0	0	0	0	0	0	2	2	2
85+	0	0	0	0	1	0	0	0	0	2	2
Totals	214	308	355	504	546	613	729	742	798	951	993

Appendix B

Female Population of Barrow, Alaska at Eleven Census Dates

Age Groups	Population at Census Date										
	1940	1944	1946	1950	1951	1954	1957	1958	1962	1966	1970
0-4	33	41	55	91	109	104	110	98	140	155	92
5-9	31	41	42	61	64	95	116	121	114	153	180
10-14	31	35	42	60	60	56	82	90	106	124	137
15-19	20	31	37	53	59	67	62	60	76	99	120
20-24	13	23	31	47	46	47	55	59	53	67	85
25-29	14	19	21	32	37	46	45	44	36	55	51
30-34	11	18	23	29	28	30	41	42	38	38	40
35-39	12	9	13	26	27	24	27	28	37	37	38
40-44	3	10	6	18	19	27	26	28	23	34	37
45-49	3	4	5	13	12	15	26	29	25	23	27
50-54	8	7	7	3	7	12	10	9	24	27	23
55-59	7	8	7	7	7	3	8	10	7	17	26
60-64	7	6	10	10	8	7	5	8	9	8	15
65-69	3	5	4	5	7	8	7	5	5	6	8
70-74	1	2	1	5	4	5	8	11	7	8	2
75-79	0	0	1	1	0	3	3	3	7	6	7
80-84	0	0	0	0	0	0	2	2	2	4	4
85+	0	0	0	0	0	0	0	0	0	0	2
Totals	197	259	305	461	494	549	633	647	709	861	894

Rural and Urban Omaha Indian Fertility

By Margot Liberty,[1] David V. Hughey[1] and Richard Scaglion[1]

ABSTRACT

A 1972 survey of fertility among 98 Omaha Indian women of childbearing age living in rural and urban areas of Nebraska shows that the urban experience has not depressed either fertility levels or the desire for large numbers of children. Larger numbers of children were desired and produced by city women than by their reservation counterparts. For other socio-economic and cultural variables such as age, education, income, and preservation of cultural traditions, the populations were comparable. High fertility cannot be explained by religious background, ignorance of, or unwillingness to use birth control. Values placed upon large families are probably related to past and present experiences of high loss rates among those children conceived and born.

Despite recent designation of American Indians as "the fastest growing ethnic group in the nation" (Time, 1970) baseline data concerning specific American Indian populations is scarce, and the overall Indian population picture, past and present, is both dim and controversial (Dobyns, 1966; Wax, 1971). Neither the Bureau of Indian Affairs nor the Bureau of the Census can say with any certainty how many Indians exist today or where, least of all in the cities where problems of definition and identification are extremely complex. Given the growing awareness of world population problems, it seemed useful to collect population data from one tribe well known to us (Liberty, 1974, 1975; Wood and Liberty, 1974) focusing upon fertility and associated variables.

The Omaha Indians, today numbering about 2,600, have lived for 300 years in an area bordering the west bank of the Missouri River in northeastern Nebraska. They were given a large reservation in 1854 and individual land allotments in the 1860's. About half the Omahas presently live there, the remainder having moved elsewhere, mostly to nearby cities, in the general wave of Indian urban migration following World War II (Bureau of Indian Affairs, 1967).

Despite many changes, the Omahas have resisted assimilation into wider American society, constituting today a viable ethnic group with distinct aspects of continuing cultural tradition. English is spoken by all, but more than half continue to speak Omaha as well. The ten traditional clans remain important, regulating marriage and social behavior and

[1]University of Pittsburgh, Pittsburgh, Pennsylvania.

providing Indian names for children. Native institutions such as powwows, handgames, and the Native American Church remain strong and vital. Those people living in the cities are generally as conservative in these respects as their reservation counterparts, tending to reinforce their Indian .identity by joining a number of new Indian organizations which have recently evolved there (Liberty, 1974).

MATERIALS AND METHODS

During the summer of 1972, rural and urban Omaha women of childbearing age (15-45) were interviewed using a questionnaire designed by an international team of experts working in collaboration with the Population Division of the United Nations (United Nations, 1970). In the rural community of Macy, the administrative center of the reservation, about 375 eligible women were available. By random sampling of a list provided by local health officials, 100 names were drawn from which 51 interviews were eventually obtained. For the urban sample, we attempted to contact all Omaha households in Lincoln and Omaha, about 35 in each city. Some households could not be contacted despite several efforts, but the total urban sample of 47 approached 68% of the Lincoln households and 51% of those in Omaha. While the overall sample of 98 interviews does not represent the entire population of present day Omahas—non-Nebraskan emigrants were not included, nor was the Omaha enclave at Sioux City, Nebraska—it is felt that the three communities surveyed yielded adequately representative samples. Some potential interview subjects in the cities were unavailable as were some on the reservation, either through absence or unwillingness to participate, but such instances were relatively few and without systematic bias.

RESULTS

Socio-economic and Cultural Characteristics

In general, the reservation and city women interviewed were similar in age, education, income, and retention of traditional custom, as shown in Table 1. Respondents averaged 33.8 years of age, 33.3 on the reservation and 34.3 in the cities. The mean number of years of school completed was 9.55, 9.88 for rural women and 9.19 for urban. Reported family income was low, averaging $440 per month on the reservation and $392 in the cities.

Retention of traditional Omaha culture continues to be strong among city dwellers. 89% were enrolled members of the tribe, as against 100% of

Table 1

Socio-economic and Cultural Characteristics

	Macy	Combined Cities
Respondent's Age (years)	33.3	34.3
Enrollment in Omaha Tribe	100%	89.4%
Mean Years of School completed	9.88	9.19
Mean Monthly Family income	$440	$392
Median Monthly Family income	$382	$397
Per cent speaking English as first language	88.2%	95.7%
Per cent still speaking Omaha	54%	60%
No. of Powwows attended	1.5	1.2
Per cent attending handgames	74%	92%
Per cent attending Native American Church	45%	45%
Per cent attending Indian Organizations	2%	60%
Per cent wearing some Indian items of dress	20%	23%

those on the reservation. English was spoken as a first language by nearly everyone, but on the reservation 54% reported using Omaha as a second language whereas 60% in the cities did so. In addition to language retention, other measures of traditional identity included participation in handgames, powwows, the Native American Church and Indian organizations, and the presence or absence of Indian items of dress. In all areas except attendance at powwows (which is explained by the lesser accessibility of powwows for city residents) the city women appear to be as interested in maintaining traditional identity as the reservation women. The high figure for participation in Indian organizations reflects the new development of such groups as Indian Centers in the cities (see Liberty, 1974 for discussion of these groups and their function).

Family, Residence, Age at Marriage

Traditional Omaha society was based upon patrilineal descent, i.e. a child belonged to his father's descent group, which named him and

Table 2

Family and Residence

	Macy	Combined Cities
Respondent's Principal Residence to Age 20		
Omaha Reservation or Bordering Community	88.3%	40.5%
Lincoln or Omaha, Nebraska	7.8%	48.9%
Other	3.9%	10.7%
Early Postmarital Residence		
Neolocal	38.6%	45%
With or near wife's family	34.1%	22.5%
With or near husband's family	25%	30%
Other	2%	2.5%
Family Type		
Nuclear	64.7%	69.6%
Extended	35.3%	21.7%
Other	0	8.7%
Family Composition		
Indian man + woman ± offspring	74.5%	57.4%
Non Indian man, Indian woman ± offspring	3.9%	17.0%
Indian mother ± offspring	19.6%	21.3%
Other	2%	4.3%

governed much of his social behavior. Residence at marriage was however matrilocal: a couple generally lived in the earth lodge of the woman's family much of the year, and extended families were common. Modern Omaha society has changed considerably from these old patterns, as shown in Table 2. Neolocal residence for newly married couples has become the norm. Reservation and city women reported roughly equivalent circumstance of residence just after marriage, with the largest number (42%) living independently.

Family type (nuclear vs. extended) and family composition (extent of intermarriage or nonmarriage) were also generally similar although marriages to non-Indian men were more common in the cities.

Table 3

Age of Respondent at Marriage

	Macy	Combined Cities
Average age	21.58	21.73
% Married, Age 13-15	6.7	0
% Married, Age 16-19	51.1	43.2
% Married, Age 20-24	22.2	29.7
% Married, Age 25-29	6.7	16.2
% Married, Age 30-34	4.4	8.1
% Married, Age 35-39	4.4	2.7
% Married, Age 40-44	4.4	0

On the whole, while differences existed in these areas, the situation of reservation and urban respondents appeared to be comparable. This and other areas of similarity may be partially explained by the relatively short period of urban experience for many Omahas who have moved into the cities; i.e. a generation or less has existed there.

Age at marriage, a major factor affecting fertility in many populations, is shown in Table 3. Omaha women have generally married by age 21 or 22, both on the reservation and in town.

Family Planning

In all three Omaha communities, large numbers of children were desired, boys being only slightly favored over girls. Urban Omahas clearly wanted even larger families than did reservation Omahas. When asked how many children they would like to have if they could start all over again, respondents from Macy, on the average, wanted 3.91 while respondents from the cities wanted 4.53. When asked what would be the ideal number of children for a tribal family (not necessarily for themselves) respondents felt that even more children would be desirable. These results are summarized in Table 4.

Once optimal family size is reached, Omaha women are amenable to the idea of delaying or preventing pregnancies through use of birth control, as shown in Table 5.

Of the respondents who favored birth control, most gave economic, social, and ideological reasons. The family economic situation, the ability to care for the child now and later, family happiness, and the feeling that the

Table 4

Ideal Number of Children (averages for all respondents)

	Macy	Combined Cities
For one's own family	3.91	4.53
For a tribal family	4.33	4.82

couple already had enough children were all valid considerations in a decision to delay or prevent further pregnancies. But freedom for the mother to work, and the belief that a small population is good for the country, were generally not considered sufficient cause.

The residents of Macy and Lincoln who disapproved of birth control most often did so for moral or medical reasons, e.g. the belief that it is harmful to health. In Omaha, respondents also cited the desire to have a large family, the feeling that a large population is good for the country, and the disapproval of their husbands.

Apparently the husband's attitude is a factor in the actual practicing of birth control methods. As shown by comparing Table 5 and 6, fewer husbands were thought to approve of birth control than the respondents themselves.

Those women who decided against the use of birth control did not do so out of ignorance. Respondents were quite sophisticated about contraceptive techniques, only three claiming no knowledge. Thus, Omaha couples are making choices about family planning based upon moral, social, and economic considerations rather than through ignorance of modern birth control technology.

Table 5

Attitude Towards Birth Control

	Macy	Combined Cities
Approve	51.0%	59.6%
Disapprove	33.3%	27.7%
Uncertain	15.7%	12.8%

Table 6

Husband's Attitude Towards Birth Control (As reported by respondent)

	Macy	Combined Cities
Approves	27.5%	29.8%
Disapproves	37.3%	31.9%
Uncertain	35.3%	38.4%

The actual use of birth control methods seems to be fairly common in all three of the communities surveyed. When asked to estimate the number of people in their communities using birth control, responses were as given in Table 7.

When asked whether they themselves had used birth control methods in the past, about half had done so while half had not (Table 8). The pill was by far the most common birth control method in all three communities. Interuterine devices were also used in Macy and Omaha.

Attitudes towards ending pregnancies through abortion were quite similar in all three Omaha communities. The great majority of respondents approved of abortion when the health of the mother was endangered, when there were serious reasons to believe the child would be deformed, and when the woman had been raped. Other reasons were generally thought to be insufficient, as shown in Table 9. Not a single woman admitted to having undergone an abortion herself.

In summary, it may be concluded that the higher fertility rates of urban Omaha women are not due to differing attitudes towards abortion or birth

Table 7

Estimate of Number of People Using Birth Control in the Respondent's Community

Respondent's Estimate	Macy	Combined Cities
Many	29.4%	36.2%
Some	45.1%	40.4%
None	3.9%	6.4%
Don't know	21.6%	17.0%

Table 8

Respondents' Past Use of Birth Control Methods

	Macy	Combined Cities
Respondent had used birth control methods	45.1%	53.2%
Respondent had *not* used birth control methods	51.0%	44.7%
Inappropriate or no response	3.9%	2.1%

Table 9

Attitude Toward Abortion

Reason for Abortion	Attitude toward Abortion for this reason	Macy	Combined Cities
The pregnancy seriously en-dangers the mother's health	Approve	74.5%	85.1%
	Disapprove	17.6%	12.8%
	Uncertain	7.9%	2.1%
There are serious reasons to believe the child will be de-formed	Approve	68.6%	66.0%
	Disapprove	21.6%	25.5%
	Uncertain	9.8%	8.5%
The woman has been raped	Approve	52.9%	57.4%
	Disapprove	29.4%	23.4%
	Uncertain	17.7%	19.1%
The couple cannot afford another child	Approve	29.4%	29.8%
	Disapprove	51.0%	63.8%
	Uncertain	19.6%	6.4%
The woman is not married	Approve	17.6%	19.1%
	Disapprove	60.8%	68.1%
	Uncertain	21.6%	12.8%
The couple does not want another child	Approve	23.5%	14.9%
	Disapprove	68.6%	76.6%
	Uncertain	7.9%	8.5%

control nor ignorance of birth control methods. In fact, respondents in the city of Omaha were more inclined to accept the idea of family planning than were respondents on the reservation. The difference in fertility is partially explained by the fact that urban Omaha women want more children than do reservation women. Once they have attained the desired number of children, family limitation is practiced by at least half of the women concerned.

Demography

Demographic data, presented in Table 10, covers three general areas: pregnancies, births, and survival. Little difference was found between the total number of pregnancies per woman among the three research communities. Total pregnancies per woman averaged 4.94 at Macy and 4.85 in the cities. Women with five or more pregnancies were common: 45.1% of the Macy sample and 51% of the city sample. City women were also having children at shorter intervals than were reservation women, but the open birth interval (time elapsed since birth of most recent child) was greater. This situation may indicate willingness of urban women to utilize birth control once desired family numbers are attained, but not before.

Table 10

Pregnancies, Births, and Survival

	Macy	Combined Cities
Average Age of Respondent	33.3	34.3
Total pregnancies per Respondent	4.94	4.85
% of Women with 5 or more pregnancies	45.1	51.1
Average years between births	3.42	2.09
Average years since most recent birth	5.56	6.45
Live births per year of marriage	.474	.420
Ratio, Live Births to pregnancies	88.89	91.23
Live Births per Respondent	4.39	4.43
% of Respondents reporting miscarriage	14.9	21
% of Respondents reporting stillbirths	8	4
Total % reporting fetal loss	22	26
Infant mortalities per thousand	40	62
Child mortality per thousand	14	10
Living Children per Respondent aged 20-40	3.24	3.89

Live births per year of marriage for the three communities averaged 448: .474 on the reservation and .420 in the cities. 90% of the pregnancies reported concluded in live births, 88.9% at Macy and 91.2% in the cities, representing a high level of fetal loss. The number of live births per woman, despite such loss, was high; 4.39 on the reservation and 4.43 in the cities. Many of these women (averaging 33 to 34 years of age) had at least ten child-bearing years ahead of them, so that these numbers could well be expected to increase unless preventive measures are indeed being taken.

About 1/4 of the women interviewed had experienced fetal loss. In Macy, 22% reported such losses, 15% due to miscarriage and 8% to stillbirth. In the cities, losses were higher: 26% reported fetal loss, with more miscarriage (21%) but less stillbirth (4%). Fetal loss thus appears to occur at an earlier stage of pregnancy in the cities than on the reservation, correlating with poorer general medical and specifically prenatal care as reported elsewhere (Sheps, 1964).

Infant mortality rates, reflecting deaths of liveborn children prior to 1 year of age, were 40 per thousand at the Macy reservation. The cities had a combined rate of 62 per thousand. Child mortality, deaths between 1 and 6 years of age, was somewhat higher on the reservation where 14 deaths per thousand were reported. The cities had a combined rate of 10 per thousand.

Nearly 2/3 of the respondents were in the key childbearing years between 20 and 40 years of age. Macy women in this age bracket averaged 3.24 living children while city women averaged 3.89. Again we have evidence of continuing high fertility in the urban setting. Numbers of children among Omaha women in the cities have not to date fallen lower than those of the reservation; to the contrary, they are higher.

DISCUSSION

Omaha Indians, recently migrating into the Nebraska cities of Lincoln and Omaha 100 miles or more from their reservation in Thurston County, may be seen as one example of a new order of "first generation American" in urban situations: urbanizing American Indians. The Omahas constitute a small but clearly defined ethnic minority in these Nebraska cities retaining as they do many aspects of traditional culture, including language, social organization (e.g. named patrilineal clans), religion (the Native American Church), and forms of recreation (powwows and handgames).

The present study, designed to compare the fertility of Omaha women in the two cities with that of women remaining on the reservation, substantiates earlier findings concerning the similarity between reservation and urban Omaha culture (Liberty, 1974). Although according to the most recent count slightly more than half of the enrolled members of the tribe remain on the reservation (Bureau of Indian Affairs, 1967), a generation or so of urban life for some has apparently created few major cultural differences. It appears that urban Omahas in Nebraska are making an effort to preserve their traditional heritage, and that in some areas (e.g. Omaha language retention and handgame attendance) they are even more traditional than reservation residents. Additionally, in the cities, new organizations stressing Indian identity (most importantly, urban Indian Centers) have sprung up and are widely belonged to. Urban Omahas are thus aware of and are interested in preserving their Indian background; and proximity to their reservation assists them in this endeavor.

Numbers of urban women available for interviewing were small, and in order to keep a balance between urban and rural respondents we only interviewed a small number at Macy also: statistical comparison must therefore be used with caution. Nonetheless, the major finding of this study—that even higher numbers of children are desired and produced by urban, as compared to reservation women—is clear. We are dealing with a society in transition from rural (reservation) to urban life, a transition characteristic of much of the rest of the world, and very characteristic of American Indians (Wax, 1972). Our study examines this process in its early stages: only half our city respondents had spent their own childhood and youth in town; the other half had arrived more recently. It seems clear, however, that city experience up to and including a whole lifetime in town has not yet depressed the desire for large numbers of children, a desire which has led them in fact to produce even more children than their reservation relatives, and to state that more children would be the ideal number if one could begin one's family all over again. This is an unusual finding in view of reports concerning urban migrants elsewhere in the world (e.g. Bogue, 1969; Davis and Cassis, 1946; DeJong, 1972; Robinson, 1963).

Explanations for continuing high production of, and desire for, children do not, as suggested elsewhere (Liberty, 1975), seem to involve conventional religious factors, anymore than they involve ignorance of or prejudice against birth control. Nor do they relate to particularly early marriage: many Omaha respondents were not married before age 21. Catholicism, often cited as a major influence in the desire for large families, is of little relevance here: Catholic missions have never existed on the Omaha reservation, and both reservation and urban Omahas belong to other Christian denominations (if any). And certainly, Omaha women, by and large, are neither ignorant of, nor averse to, the use of birth control. Only three of 98 women interviewed professed ignorance of birth control methods; and a large majority in each community approved of their use, close to 50% having employed them themselves. It would appear then that reasons for the high Omaha desire for, and production of, children must be sought beyond these conventional explanations.

Possible explanations for high Omaha fertility may perhaps be most fruitfully sought in two areas: Omaha experience retained in tribal memory; and present Omaha experience as it continues to develop in the welfare economy which is prevalent both on the reservation and in the cities. As reported elsewhere, staggering population loss was experienced by the Omaha tribe during 19th century epidemics of contagious disease (Wood and Liberty, 1974; Liberty, 1975). The Omaha were nearly exterminated by smallpox in 1802, losing perhaps 1500 to 2000 people. Smallpox killed 300 of the survivors in 1837 and cholera 500 more in 1849; subsequent measles epidemics before 1900 killed more than 200. To survive at all under such conditions, the Omaha birth rate must have been phenomenal; and attitudes favoring high numbers of children as an instrument of personal as well as cultural survival may well have filtered down to the present day. The Omaha population reached a low of about 800 after the 1849 cholera, but it has steadily increased since that time.

Modern Omaha experience may well be reinforcing high family-size values for other reasons (which incidentally beg for further research concerning personal decision making). Documentation of the perceived economic value of children to parents under modern circumstances is not available from the present study. High expectation of fetal loss and/or infant and child mortality is however clearly present in view of the facts that one out of four Omaha women have experienced miscarriage or stillbirth, and that many others have lost young children as well. In the delicate and rapidly changing adjustments of the welfare economy shared by so many American Indians with the rest of the nation's poor, Indian women may well regard the conception of a number of children, some of whom will probably die, as their best form of social security. Once sufficient numbers of children (to the Omaha way of thinking) have been produced, the birth of further children is deliberately prevented.

ACKNOWLEDGEMENTS

Field research for the project reported here was supported by the Center for Population Research of the National Institute of Child Health and Human Development (Research Grant 1-R01-HD-06129-01). Analysis was supported by a Faculty Research Grant from the College of Arts and Sciences, and by the Provost's Research Development Fund of the University of Pittsburgh. We also thank Janet Goldenstein Ahler, Pauline Tyndall, and Shirley Cayou (fieldwork phase) and Judith R. Baker, Sherry Y. Ellison, and Catherine Marshall (analysis and write up phase).

Received: 19 May 1975.

Literature Cited

Bogue, D. J.   1969   Principles of demography. John Wiley, New York.

Bureau of Indian Affairs   1967   Omaha tribe. Report of the Superintendent of Winnebago Agency, 1966. Washington.

Davis K. and A. Casis   1946   Urbanization in Latin America. Milbank Memorial Fund Quart. **24**: 186-207.

DeJong, G.F.   1972   Patterns of human fertility and mortality. *In:* The structure of human populations, G. A. Harris and A. J. Boyce (Eds.); Clarendon Press, Oxford, pp. 32-56.

Dobyns, H. F.   1966   Estimating Aboriginal American population: An appraisal of techniques with a new hemispheric estimate. Current Anthropology 7: 395-449.

Liberty, M.   1974   The urban reservation. Ph.D Dissertation, University of Minnesota, Minneapolis.

───── 1975   Population trends among present day Omaha Indians. Plains Anthropologist. In press.

Robinson, W. C.   1963   Urbanization and fertility: The non-Western experience. Milbank Memorial Fund Quart. 41: 291-308.

Sheps, M. C.   1964   Pregnancy wastage as a factor in the analysis of fertility data. Demography 11: 111-118.

Time   1970   Goodbye to Tonto. February 9, pp. 14-20.

Wax, M. L.   1971   Indian Americans: Unity and diversity. Prentice Hall, Englewood Cliffs, N.J.

Wood, W. R. and M. Liberty   1975   Omaha. Handbook of North American Indians 11. Smithsonian Institution, Washington. In press.

Hepatitis B Surface Antigen, Fertility and Sex Ratio: Implications for Health Planning[1]

By J. E. Hesser,[2] B. S. Blumberg[2] and J. S. Drew[2]

ABSTRACT

Matings with a parent positive for infectious agent (HB$_s$Ag) in a Greek population show an elevated sex ratio (64% males) compared with matings of negative parents (53% males). In Melanesian populations, however, the sex ratio is decreased when the mother is positive and increased when the father is positive. Thus the presence of HB$_s$Ag is associated with alterations in the live birth sex ratio. Altered sex ratios, in turn, affect population reproduction rates.

This paper will discuss an infectious disease agent associated with fertility expression. We believe these studies demonstrate that biologic components of fertility, along with cultural-behavioral ones, warrant consideration in the development of policies of disease and population control (e.g. the World Fertility Survey currently underway has in general excluded consideration of biologic factors in its assessment of fertility determinants in different parts of the world).

Policies for the control of infectious disease are generally concerned with decreasing mortality and/or morbidity from specific causes. Disease control is a major factor in demographic change because of reductions in mortality. Indirect and direct effects on fertility also occur (e.g. smallpox, tuberculosis, malaria, syphilis, toxoplasmosis, and rubella affect pregnancies and the chances for their successful termination). We discuss here a specific example of an infectious agent which can be controlled by public health measures, and which is also associated with changes in fertility expression, specifically, changes in the sex ratio of livebirths.

Hepatitis B surface antigen, or HB$_s$Ag (originally called Australia antigen or Au) is associated with an infectious agent which causes acute and

[1]This work was supported in part by USPHS grants CA-06551, RR-05539 and CA-06927 from the National Institutes of Health and by an appropriation from the Commonwealth of Pennsylvania. A portion of the work is part of a research project of the Peabody Museum and Department of Anthropology, Harvard University, supported by Grant No. GM-13482 of the National Institute of General Medical Sciences, USPHS; it is also part of the Human Adaptability Section of the International Biological Program, and was conducted with the permission and kind assistance of the Administration of the British Solomon Islands Protectorate.

[2]The Institute for Cancer Research, The Fox Chase Cancer Center, Philadelphia, Pennsylvania, 19111.

chronic "viral" hepatitis in man and is also associated with other diseases, including primary cancer of the liver, leukemia, and leprosy.[3] HB_sAg may be the surface coat of a hepatitis virus, but in this chapter, when the term HB_sAg is used, it is used to refer to the infectious agent. HB_sAg occurs in the blood of some people who are carriers and who can infect others but who are themselves not ill, as well as in the blood of people with hepatitis. The prevalence of HB_sAg carriers varies from population to population, for example, from 0.1% in the general U.S. population, to 20% or more in some Pacific populations. Several specificities of the antigen have been identified, and populations can be characterized by antigen subtypes as well as by prevalence (Mazzur et al. 1973).

The antigen is transmitted in blood (e.g. by transfusion) and may also be transmitted by the fecal-oral route, by droplet infection, and by vectors such as clams and mosquitoes. There is also evidence that vertical transmission from parent to child occurs (Mazzur et al. 1974). The antigen can be detected in blood serum using immunodiffusion, but more sensitive tests, such as radioimmunoassay, passive-hemagglutination inhibition, and counterelectrophoresis, are usually used.

Decreasing the prevalence of HB_sAg in a population may be accomplished in a number of ways. For example, decreasing the opportunities for transmission of the agent by screening of bloods used for transfusions has decreased the incidence of post-transfusion hepatitis in this country considerably. It has been conjectured that control of HB_sAg, possibly through vaccination, in areas where the carrier frequency is high, may eventually result in a decline in chronic liver disease and hepatoma in those areas. These diseases are major causes of morbidity and death in Africa and Asia, where HB_sAg is common. It is clear that there could be health benefits resulting from measures which decrease the prevalence of HB_sAg in many populations. There may also be other effects of decreasing the prevalence of this infectious agent, because it is also related to fertility expression.

Studies by a number of investigators of HB_sAg have focused upon the characteristics of families whose members are and are not carriers of the antigen (Blumberg, et al. 1966; Ceppelini et al. 1970; Helske, 1974; Szmuness et al. 1973; Stevens et al. 1975). The studies described here tested the hypothesis that there is a relation between the HB_sAg carrier status of parents, their fertility, and the sex ratio of their offspring.

---

[3]A summary description of hepatitis B surface antigen can be found in a number of sources, including Blumberg and Hesser (1975).

The most significant results of these studies concerned the sex ratio of reported livebirths. Sex ratio is defined as the number of males times 100, divided by the number of females.) Results on the number of offspring will be only reviewed briefly.

MATERIALS AND METHODS

The methods used to detect the presence of HB_sAg in sera include: immunodiffusion (London, 1973), reaction electrophoresis (Gocke and Howe, 1970), radioimmunoassay by a modification of the method of Purcell et al. (1973), and passive-hemagglutination inhibition by the Hepanosticon (Organon) method.

An initial study was carried out using genealogic data and sera collected in 1968 by Dr. J. Friedlaender of Harvard University, on Bougainville, Papua New Guinea (Kahn et al. 1972). The sera had been tested for HB_sAg by immunodiffusion and 9.16% of the population were identified as carriers. In a matched pair study, with 20 mothers in each group matched for age and village, comparisons of the number and sex of reported offspring were made between categories of matings. Three categories of matings were distinguished: 1. mother HB_sAg positive (+) and father HB_sAg negative (0); 2. father (+) and mother (0); 3. both mother and father (0). This study showed that families with positive fathers were significantly larger than others, and that families with positive mothers had a noticeably, though not significantly, decreased number of males in their offspring. The sex ratio of offspring in matings with positive mothers was 77 (43.5% males); it was 108 (53% males) in the other matings.

These initial observations on the Bougainville population stimulated development of another study, subsequently carried out in a region of Greece where the prevalence of HB_sAg was known to be 5% or greater. This study was specifically designed to test the hypothesis that there was an alteration of fertility, and a distortion of sex ratio, associated with the presence of HB_sAg in parents. It is described in detail in a recent paper (Hesser et al. 1975) and the results are summarized here.

Approximately 70% of the population of a village in Greek Macedonia was studied. One thousand and ninety eight people had their sera tested for HB_sAg by radioimmunoassay and other methods. The prevalence of HB_sAg carriers in the population was 11.3%.

From this population matings were selected in which both parents had been tested and the same three categories of matings were distinguished as before. There were 27 matings with the mother (+), 20 with the father (+) and 172 with both parents (0).

The hypothesis that the sex ratio is altered in families in which one or another parent is HB_sAg (+) was also tested using data from several Melanesian populations. The data had been collected by the late Dr. A. Damon, and Drs. W. Howells and D. Oliver, and a team of investigators sponsored by Harvard University. It was made available to us by the Department of Anthropology at Harvard University. Data from three Solomon Island populations were used. These populations included the Aita, living on Bougainville Island (but not included in Dr. Friedlaender's study); the Lau, living on Malaita, and the Baegu, also living on Malaita. These are all rural Melanesian populations though the environments they occupy differ from one another. The Aita live at high altitude; the Lau on a coastal lagoon, and the Baegu in a low altitude, inland area.

The sera of about 90% of each of these populations (or around 400 persons in each) were tested for HB_sAg by immunodiffusion. The carrier rates were very high in each of them—19.6% among the Aita, 25% among the Lau, and 16.5% among the Baegu.

The data from each of these populations were treated in the same way as that from Greece. That is, mating types were identified according to the carrier status of the parents. In the combined populations there were 45 matings with the mother (+), 21 with the father (+), and 115 with both parents (0).

RESULTS

In an analysis which controlled for mothers' ages, differences in fertility between these mating groups could not be distinguished in either the Greek or the Melanesian populations using Scheffe F projections to test for differences between the means of multiple groups (Miller, 1967). In the Greek population, in an analysis which controlled for mothers' age and for differences in sample sizes of the mating groups, the sex ratio of offspring in matings with a positive parent (i.e. categories 1 and 2 combined) was significantly (p<.025) increased, compared with that for matings of negative parents. In matings with a positive parent, the sex ratio was 185 (64% males); in matings with negative parents, the sex ratio was 112 (53% of males) (Table 1).

In each of the three Melanesian populations, the number and sex of offspring of the three mating types were compared with one another, controlling for mothers' age. In each of these populations, alterations in sex ratio of livebirths were seen. A decreased sex ratio was observed in matings with HB_sAg positive mothers, and an elevation of sex ratio in matings with

Table 1

Sex Ratio of Offspring from Matings of Parents with and without HB$_s$Ag in a Greek Population

| | Number of Mothers | Number of Offspring | | |
		Male	Female	Sex Ratio
mother HB$_s$Ag(+)	27	49	28	175
father HB$_s$Ag (+)	20	36	18	200
Total, either parent HB$_s$Ag (+)	47	85	46	185
parents HB$_s$Ag(0)	172	287	255	112

positive fathers, when these matings were compared with matings of negative parents. The same kind of observation had been made in the Bougainville study (Table 2). The data from these four Melanesian populations (the three new ones and the earlier Bougainville study) showed alterations in livebirth sex ratio associated with HB$_s$Ag carrier status of parents that were similar. When treated independently, the data from each population does not yield a statistically significant result. However, the probability of observing by chance sex ratio alterations of the same kind (e.g. decreased when the mother is HB$_s$Ag positive and elevated when the father is positive) in each of four populations is less than .01, according to the multiplicative law of probability. In addition, when the data for these four Melanesian populations is pooled, the decreased proportion of males in matings with positive mothers is significantly different (p<.02) from matings either with the father positive, or with both parents negative. The elevated sex ratio associated with HB$_s$Ag in the father is not significantly distinguishable from matings with both parents negative when the data are pooled (Table 3).

DISCUSSION

One conclusion from these studies is that the presence of an infectious agent (HB$_s$Ag) in parents is biologically associated with an alteration in the livebirth sex ratio of their offspring. This conclusion has biological and demographic implications.

Table 2

Sex Ratio of Offspring from Matings of Parents with and without HB_sAg, in four Melanesian Populations. (Mos. = Mothers   SR = Sex ratio)

	Aita			Lau			Baegu			Bougainville		
	No. Mos.	♂♂/♀♀	SR	No. Mos.	♂♂/♀♀	SR	No. Mos.	♂♂/♀♀	SR	No. Mos.	♂♂/♀♀	SR
Mother $HB_sAg(+)$	12	24/35	69	21	23/26	89	12	17/26	65	21	54/70	77
Father $HB_sAg(+)$	14	28/26	108	5	14/6	233	2	3/0	233	20	51/47	109
Parents $HB_sAg(0)$	37	70/84	83	33	65/72	90	45	75/69	109	226	593/552	107

Table 3

Sex Ratio of Offspring from Matings of Parents with and without HB₅Ag, in pooled Data from Four Melanesian Populations

	Number of Offspring		
	Male	Female	Sex Ratio
Mother HB$_s$Ag(+)	118	157	75
Father HB$_s$Ag(+)	96	79	123
Parents HB$_s$Ag(0)	803	777	103

First, if the prevalence of the infectious agent (assuming that it is directly related to the sex ratio change) is altered in a population, what impact upon population structure could this have?

The effect of different sex ratios upon population reproduction rates was calculated using a model presented by M. Teitelbaum (in Harrison and Boyce, 1973). This model assumes unchanged age-specific birth and female mortality rates, and variable sex ratio, in calculating the net reproduction rate and the rate of increase of the stable population. (The net reproduction rate indicates the rate at which a cohort of women replace themselves, or the size of the second generation of females, given certain birth and mortality schedules. The stable population is a demographic model representing the permanent structure that a hypothetical population would have if assumed age-specific birth and death rates did not change over time. Such models are used to show the implications of changes in specified conditions of populations). Teitelbaum's data for number of births and female mortality were used. Sex ratios used were based on data from our Greek village study.

The livebirth sex ratio for the total population of the Greek village was 115. If the contribution of HB$_s$Ag parents is not included, the livebirth sex ratio is 107. The net reproduction rates for two populations, with these livebirth sex ratios, are different and equivalent to a difference between a replacement of 1000 females by 1,620 versus 1,680. The rate of increase of the population with a sex ratio of 107 is 3.87% higher than that of one with a sex ratio of 115. In terms of population doubling, if a generation estimate of 25.87 years is used (the estimate used with Teitelbaum's data), this would mean a difference between 37 and 34 years. This demonstrates that the effect of a precisely identifiable biological characteristic of the population (the prevalence of the infectious agent associated with HB$_s$Ag) could be measurable. Factors affecting a population's sex ratio may warrant consideration along with factors directly affecting the number of births.

Second, if one infectious agent is found to be associated with the fertility expression of a segment of a population, it is reasonable to think that similar effects may be related to other infectious agents. The analytic study of population growth requires the identification of individual factors which have measurable effects.

The third implication of the observations presented here concerns the interdependence of social organization and the demographic characteristics of populations. An example given by Mazzur and Watson (1974) reports an excess of males among the siblings of HB_sAg carriers on Santa Cruz in the Solomon Islands. There is an excess of males living on Santa Cruz. In addition, there is a higher mortality among women of childbearing age. Men commonly marry more than once. Excess women are available for marriage on the Reef Islands, and then are brought to Santa Cruz as brides. Formalized trade relations exist between these islands in which there is one way travel of women from the Reef Islands to Santa Cruz in exchange for bride prices of red feather money and food. This exchange is basic to the economy and trade relationships of the entire island group. The shortage of women on Santa Cruz, due in part (perhaps) to the excess number of males in HB_sAg families, enhances this trade. The removal of women to Santa Cruz from the Reef Islands limits population expansion in those resource-limited islands. Thus, the economy of an entire island group may be affected to some degree by the interaction of an infectious agent (the one associated with HB_sAg) with these populations.

The social organization of human populations is dependent, in part, upon the proportion and distribution by age of males and females. Our observations indicate that the sex ratio of a population could be related to its interaction with other organisms (infectious agents) in the environment, as well as to other biologic factors; the balance of these interactions could be significant in the maintenance of social organization, and for the character of population growth.

The observation of an alteration in livebirth sex ratio associated with HB_sAg, but in different directions in the Greek and in the Melanesian populations has been made. It is intriguing to consider that the presence of HB_sAg in a parent is associated with a disturbance in sex ratio, and that other factors determine the expression of the alteration.

Received: 28 May 1975.

LITERATURE CITED

BLUMBERG, B. S. AND J. E. HESSER 1975 Anthropology and infectious disease. *In:* Physiological anthropology, A. Damon and J. Friedlaender (editors), Oxford University Press, Oxford.

BLUMBERG, B. S., L. MELARTIN, R. A. GUINTO AND B. WERNER 1966 Family studies of a human serum isoantigen system (Australia antigen). Am. J. Hum. Genet. **18:** 594-608.

CEPPELINI, R., G. BEDARIDA, A. O. CARBONARA, B. TRINCHIERI AND B. FILIPPI 1970 High frequency and family clustering of Au antigen in some Italian populations. Atti. Conv. Farmital. Antigene Australia et Epatite Virale, Minerva Med., Torino.

GOCKE, D. J. AND C. HOWE 1970 Rapid detection of Australia antigen by counterimmunoelectrophoresis. J. Immunol. **104:** 1031-1032.

HELSKE, T. 1974 Carriers of Hepatitis B antigen and transfusion hepatitis in Finland. Scandinavian J. Haematol., Supplement 22. Munksgaard, Copenhagen.

HESSER, J. E., J. ECONOMIDOU AND B. S. BLUMBERG 1975 Hepatitis-associated antigen (HB$_s$Ag) in parents and sex ratio of offspring in a Greek population. Human Biol. **47:** 415-425.

KAHN, M., W. T. LONDON AND B. S. BLUMBERG (Unpublished manuscript, 1973) Australia antigen and family size. Studies in Bougainville.

LONDON, W. T. 1973 The immunodiffusion method for the detection of Australia antigen. *In:* Australia antigen, J. E. Prier and H. Friedman (editors). University Park Press, Baltimore.

MAZZUR, S., B. S. BLUMBERG AND J. FRIEDLAENDER 1974 Silent maternal transmission of Australia antigen. Nature, **247:** 41-43.

MAZZUR, S., D. FALKER AND B. S. BLUMBERG 1973 Geographical variation of the "w" subtype of Australia antigen. Nature New Biology **243:** 44-47.

MAZZUR, S. AND T. M. WATSON 1974 Excess males among siblings of Australia antigen carriers. Nature **250:** 60-61.

MILLER, R. G. 1967 Simultaneous statistical inference. McGraw Hill, New York.

PURCELL, R. J., D. C. WONG, H. J. ALTER AND P. V. HOLLAND 1973 A microtiter solid-phase radioimmunoassay for Hepatitis B antigen. Applied Microbiol. **26:** 478-480.

STEVENS, C. E., R. P. BEASLEY, J. TSUI AND W. LEE 1975 Vertical transmission of Hepatitis B antigen in Taiwan. New Eng. J. Med. **292:** 771-774.

SZMUNESS, W., A. M. PRINCE, R. L. HIRSCH AND B. BROTMAN 1973 Familial clustering of Hepatitis B infection. New Eng. J. Med. **289:** 1162-1166.

TEITELBAUM, M. D. 1972 Factors associated with the sex ratio in human populations. *In:* The structure of human populations. G. A. Harrison and A. J. Boyce (editors) Clarendon Press, Oxford.

Altitude and Fertility

By Andrew E. Abelson[1]

ABSTRACT

Evidence from physiological studies indicates that hypoxia may act as a stress that reduces fecundity; and in human populations resident at high altitude there is evidence of reduced fertility (James, 1966). In this paper the fertility of high Andean populations is described with reference to the ecological and social context. An analysis of high Andean energy flow (Thomas, 1972) indicates that children are an economic asset, and consideration of the social organization of high Andean rural communities supports this view. A study of the fertility of migrants from high to low altitude indicates that reproductive performance increases with the removal of the stress of hypoxia (Abelson et al. 1974). It is therefore concluded that the reduced fertility observed in high Andean populations is due to the effect of hypoxia on human fecundity.

The level of fertility achieved by a population depends on its fecundity, or biological capacity to produce offspring, and the extent to which this is modified by social and cultural factors. At high altitude the stress of hypoxia may act to reduce fecundity, and in this way also reduce fertility. The purpose of this paper is to review the role of hypoxia in relation to reproductive performance in the high Andean environment.

Physiological Studies

Evidence for the physiological effect of hypoxia on fertility in both experimental animals and in human populations is described in the reviews of Clegg and Harrison (1971), Baker and Dutt (1972) and Hoff and Abelson (1976). To summarize briefly:

1. In both experimental animals and in man, sperm production may be reduced on ascent to high altitude (Donayre et al. 1968). However, this effect may only be temporary (Guerra Garcia et al. 1965).

2. Ovulation is affected in rats exposed to hypobarometric pressures (Donayre et al. 1968); the sizes of litters are reduced (Fernandez Cano, 1959); and the birth weights of offspring are low (Moore and Price, 1948). There is a lack of evidence of anovulation in women living at high altitude.

[1]Department of Anthropology, The Pennsylvania State University, University Park, Pa. 16802 USA. Present address: The University of Sussex, Arts Building, Falmer, Brighton BN1 9QN, Sussex, England.

3. In women normally resident at low altitude, travel to high altitude can result in disturbance of the menstrual cycle (Sobrevilla, 1967; Harris et al. 1966).

4. No data exist on implantation in human subjects living at high altitude, but those travelling to high altitude when pregnant may experience a greater risk of miscarriage, especially in the third trimester (Johnson and Roofe, 1965; McClung, 1969).

5. The birth weights of the newborn at high altitude are lower than those born at low altitude (Grahn and Kratchman, 1963). This effect is less, but still significant for those native to high altitude, compared to matched individuals living at low altitude (McClung, 1969; Kruger and Arias Stella, 1970; Sobrevilla, 1971; Haas, 1973).

CENSUS STUDIES

Turning to the demographic implications of the effect of hypoxia on fecundity, three questions can be formulated. 1. Can hypoxia depress fecundity sufficiently to have a significant effect on birth rates? 2. What is the magnitude of this effect? 3. To what extent would the reduced fertility of those exposed to a hypoxic stress be measurable in a national population?

During the 1960s several authors (Stycos, 1963; Heer, 1964, 1967; James, 1966; Whitehead, 1968; Bradfield, 1969) debated possible explanations for the reduced fertility observed in the high Andes, using data derived from the national censuses of Peru, Bolivia and Ecuador. While altitude emerged as a significant variable (James, 1966; Heer, 1967), it proved difficult to discriminate between the effects of hypoxia and potentially important social and cultural variables. In addition some doubts were raised as to the reliability of the data.

COMMUNITY STUDIES

In an attempt to resolve the problems raised, attention turned to the study of individuals in small communities. Suitable communities with relatively homogeneous populations and of comparable socio-economic levels were already under intensive study as part of an International Biological Program investigation of adaptation to high altitude. They include Nuñoa, whose residents live at altitudes between 4000 and 4500 meters on the south Peruvian *altiplano*, and communities in the Tambo valley at sea level in the south of Peru. In addition to the demographic data collected from these communities, our understanding of the fertility levels achieved depends on the study of subsistence requirements and energy flow in Nuñoa (Thomas, 1972) and on the social organization of the community (Escobar, 1976).

Nuñoa: A High Altitude Community

The subsistence needs of the population are met by the cultivation of potatoes and the Andean grains *quinoa* and *canihua,* and by the utilization of animal resources. Animal resources may either be used for direct consumption, or their meat, skins and wool may be traded for goods available in other ecozones (Thomas, 1972; Escobar, 1976). Such trade has a history of several centuries (Murra, 1968). The contributions of the three types of productive activity depend on the labor available to perform the duties required. In a family consisting of a married couple and four children, sales of animal products provided over three-quarters of the annual caloric intake, and the direct consumption of animal produce provided just over a quarter of the remainder (Thomas, 1972). This estimate of the input from animal resources is, however, conservative. As Thomas points out, animals provide dung for fertilizer in the fields as well as a means of transporting goods both locally and for sale elsewhere. In addition, an animal herd provides security against the loss of crops from local drought, frost or flooding (Thomas, 1972).

The labor force used in subsistence activities is related to the energetic efficiency of individuals or groups performing the tasks, and their ability to do the work. Herding activities are carried out by children whose energy costs are less (Thomas, 1972). Where animal resources are consumed directly, the energy costs of adults are hardly covered (Thomas, 1972). Concerning the economic activities of children in the Andes, Nuñez del Prado (1955) and Mishkin (1946) report that children as young as six years of age work.

The trading of animal resources is carried out by adult men, but for this activity, trading partners are required. Because of the value of trade in the family budget, it is important that trading partners are reliable; they are usually ceremonial kin relations. Such kin are most often formed at ceremonies related to the birth and development of children (Gillin, 1945).

Kin relations are also important in cultivation activities. In field preparation, the greatest energetic efficiency is obtained by the co-operation of three individuals, often a married couple and a kinsman (Thomas, 1972). This unit of three is common in the high Andes (Mishkin, 1946). But, co-operation also extends to larger numbers of individuals assisting in field preparation. Groups known as *ayni* existed in Inca times (Rowe, 1946), as well as in the present (Mishkin, 1946). The reciprocity of labor exchange depends on kin relations, and it is therefore not surprising that the Quechua word for a poor man is the same as that for a man with few kin (Escobar, 1976).

The mating system in Nuñoa is one of serial monogamy. Marriage, or the formation of a union, often follows first pregnancy; and it appears that women may be at risk to pregnancy between unions. Completed fertility in Nuñoa was 6.7 (Hoff, 1968). While this level of fertility is high by western standards, the reproductive performance of peasants living at low altitudes is often greater (Henry, 1961). In view of the lack of knowledge of contraception, the economic advantages of children, and the system of social organization, the level of fertility in Nuñoa provides negative evidence for an effect of hypoxia on reproductive performance at high altitude.

The Tambo Valley: Communities at Low Altitude

There is evidence that high fertility is favorable to Nuñoans, but those living at low altitude achieve higher levels. In order to isolate and measure the magnitude of a hypoxic effect on fertility a comparative study was undertaken by Abelson et al. (1974). The residents of the Tambo valley include not only life-time residents of the valley, but also migrants to the valley. Some of these migrants were born at high altitude, defined here as above 3000 meters, and others at low altitude. Measurement of the fertility of life-time residents of the valley provided base line data with which to compare the fertility of the Nuñoans. The fertility of the downward migrants living at low altitude provided the opportunity to examine their fertility in the absence of hypoxia. Measurement of the fertility of migrants born at low altitude made it possible to control for the effect of migration.

The data were collected by questionnaire interview, and comprise a 10% sample of the adult women in the communities studied. Analysis of the responses showed that there were some errors in the ages reported, but that 90% were accurate to within two years. The accuracy of these replies did not depend on altitude of birthplace.

Completed fertility could not be used as a measure of fertility because the migrants had lived parts of their reproductive lives in different places. Instead, the number of children born in a five-year interval, where the individual had spent all five years in the same environment, was used.

The mean age at marriage for each group of subjects in the Tambo valley was within a year of that of Nuñoa. The marriage system was also similar, one of serial monogamy. A survey of contraceptive use and knowledge indicated little application of these methods.

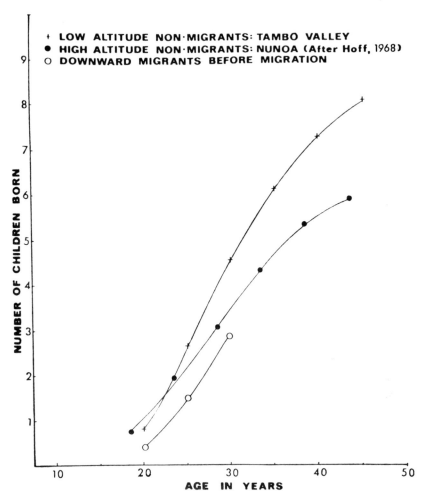

FIG. 1. Cumulative fertility of high and low altitude nonmigrant populations (after Abelson et al. 1974)

Figure 1 shows the difference in fertility between those living at high altitude in Nuñoa and the life-time residents of the Tambo valley. This illustrates the basic fertility difference between high and low altitude in terms of numbers of children born. Compared to the completed fertility of the Nuñoans, which was 6.7, completed fertility of the Tambo valley life-time residents was 8.29. While this figure of 8.29 was based on only a

Table 1

Births by Five Year Age Intervals, According to Altitude of Birthplace and Migrant Status:[1] From Reproductive Histories of Subjects living in the Tambo Valley

| | Low Altitude Born | | | | | | | | | High Altitude Born | | | | | |
| | Non-Migrant Tambo Valley | | | Migrant Before Migration | | | Migrant After Migration | | | Migrant Before Migration | | | Migrant After Migration | | |
Age Group	N	X̄	S.D.	N	X̄	S.D.	N	X̄	S.D.	N	X̄	S.D.	N	X̄	S.D.
15-19.9	56	0.79	1.02	36	0.44	0.65	19	0.95	0.91	57	0.37	0.69	23	1.08	0.99
20-24.9	54	1.87	1.23	18	1.28	1.13	30	1.70	0.99	33	1.12	1.11	39	2.00	0.75
25-29.9	44	1.89	1.20	—			34	1.65	1.07	17	1.41	1.12	38	1.76	1.10
30-34.9	34	1.53	1.37	—			29	1.34	0.97	—	—		31	1.84	1.03
35-39.9	28	1.21	1.37	—			24	1.00	1.14	—	—		21	0.14	1.01
40-44.9	16	0.75	0.86	—			19	1.05	1.47	—	—		14	0.64	1.09
Total		8.04			—			7.69			—			8.46	

[1]After Abelson et al. (1974)

very small sample, their estimated total fertility, obtained by summing age specific rates for all life-time residents of the valley, was 8.04, giving more confidence in the completed fertility measured.

This figure also shows some data for those born at high altitude, living at that altitude before they had migrated. Only data for younger ages are available due to the age specific characteristics of migrants. The reproductive lives of these individuals begun a little later than for the Nuñoans, but the similarity of the slopes indicates that rates of fertility were similar.

Table 1 describes the fertility of subjects at risk to pregnancy in the Tambo valley. Columns 1, 3, and 5, describe life-time residents, low altitude born migrants, and high altitude born migrants respectively. It can be seen that all three groups have similar fertility characteristics regardless of migrant status and altitude of birthplace. Migrants born at low altitude do show an increase in fertility with migration, but not to a level greater than life-time residents of the valley. Migrants born at high altitude were the most fertile of all those living in the valley. For these subjects the increase in fertility on migration from high to low altitude was significant at the 0.01 level for ages 15 to 19.9 and 20 to 24.9 years.

Following the comparison of pairs of population, attempts were made to see whether inter-population differences could be explained in terms of social or cultural factors. The factors examined included previous fertility history, age at marriage, age at migration, first language learned and socio-economic status. No significant relationships were found. Considering the possible effect of migration, Goldberg (1959) and Iutaka et al. (1971) provide data that suggest that migrants normally retain the fertility characteristics of their place of birth; and Mejia Valera (1963) reports that downward migrants in the Andes remain relatively unacculturated. The data presented here are therefore interpreted to show that the removal of the stress of hypoxia does allow an increase in fertility.

CONCLUSION

In conclusion, the stress of hypoxia can act to reduce fertility, and this effect is measurable at the population level. The size of the effect is between 1 and 2 births per woman, and the greatest effect appears to be in the early 20's. Greater effects could obviously be achieved by social and cultural constraints; but for the major part of the population of the high Andes, living in rural areas, hypoxia appears as the most important factor affecting fertility.

ACKNOWLEDGEMENTS

The field research which made this paper possible depends not only on the work of the authors cited, but also on many others who have collectively contributed to the International Biological Program study of high altitude populations directed by Dr. Paul T. Baker. The study of fertility in the Tambo Valley was first described in an MA thesis in Anthropology at The Pennsylvania State University, which was in part published by Abelson, Baker and Baker (1974). Financial assistance for this research was provided by The Wenner-Gren Foundation (Grant no. 2723) and NIGMS training grant no. 5 TIO GMO 1748-03.

Received: 27 March 1975.

LITERATURE CITED

ABELSON, A. E., T. S. BAKER AND P. T. BAKER   1974   Altitude, migration and fertility in the Andes. Social Biol. **21**:12-27.

BAKER, P. T. AND J. S. DUTT   1972   Demographic variables as measures of biological adaptation: A case study of high altitude human populations. *In* The structure of human populations. G. A. Harrison and A. J. Boyce (eds.) Clarendon Press, Oxford.

BRADSHAW, B. S.   1969   Fertility differences in Peru: A reconsideration. Population Studies, **23**: 5-19.

CLEGG, E. J. AND G. A. HARRISON   1971   Reproduction in human high altitude populations. Hormones, **2**: 13-25.

DONAYRE, J., R. GUERRA GARCIA, F. MONCLOA AND L. A. SOBREVILLA   1968   Endocrine studies at altitude. IV. Changes in the semen of men. J. Reprod. Fert. **16**: 55-58.

ESCOBAR, G. M.   1976   The social and political structure of Nuñoa. *In* Man in the Andes: A multidisciplinary study of high altitude Quechua. P. T. Baker and M. A. Little (eds.). In press.

FERNANDEZ CANO, L.   1959   The effects of increase or decrease of body temperature or of hypoxia on ovulation and pregnancy in the rat. *In* Recent progress in the endocrinology of reproduction. C. W. Lloyd (ed.). Academic Press, New York, pp. 97-106.

GILLIN, JOHN   1945   Moche: A Peruvian coastal community. Smithsonian Institution. Institute of Social Anthropology, Publication No. 3. Washington.

GOLDBERG, D.   1959   The fertility of two generation urbanities. Population Studies **12**: 214-222.

GRAHN, D. AND J. KRATCHMAN   1963   Variation in neonatal death rate and birthweight in the United States and possible relations to environmental radiation, geology and altitude. Am. J. Hum. Genet. **15**: 329-352.

GUERRA GARCIA, R., R. A. VELASQUEZ AND J. WHITTEMBURY   1965   Urinary testosterone in high altitude natives. Steroids **6**: 351-355.

HAAS, J. D.   1973   Altitudinal variation in infant growth and development in Peru. Ph.D. Thesis, Pennsylvania State University, University Park, Pa.

HARRIS, C., J. L. SHIELDS AND J. P. HANNON   1966   Acute altitude sickness in females. Aerospace Med. **37**: 1163-1167.

HEER, D. M. 1964 Fertility differences between Indian and Spanish speaking parts of Andean countries. Population Studies 18: 71-84.

HEER, D. M. 1967 Fertility differences in Andean countries: A reply to W. H. James. Population Studies 21: 71-73.

HENRY, L. 1961 Some data on natural fertility. Eugenics Quarterly 8: 81-91.

HOFF, C. J. AND A. E. ABELSON 1976 Fertility. *In* Man in the Andes: A multidisciplinary study of high altitude Quechua. P. T. Baker and M. A. Little (eds.). In press. No. 1, Department of Anthropology, Pennsylvania State University, University Park, Pa.

HOFF, C. J. AND A. E. ABELSON 1976 Fertility. *In* Man in the Andes: A multidisciplinary study of high altitude Quechua. P. T. Baker and M. A. Little (eds.). In press.

IUTAKA, S., E. W. BOCK AND W. G. VARNES 1971 Factors affecting fertility in natives and migrants in urban Brazil. Population Studies 25: 55-82.

JAMES, W. H. 1966 The effect of high altitude on fertility in Andean countries. Population Studies 20: 87-101.

JOHNSON, D. AND P. D. ROOFE 1965 Blood constituents of normal newborn rats and those exposed to low oxygen tension during gestation: Weight of newborn and litter size also considered. Anat. Rec. 153: 303-309.

KRUGER, H. AND J. ARIAS STELLA 1970 The placenta and the newborn infant at high altitude. Am. J. Obstet. Gynec. 106: 486-491.

McCLUNG, J. 1969 Effects of high altitude on human birth. Harvard Univ. Press. Cambridge, Mass.

MEJIA VALERA, J. 1963 Sumario sobre factores sociales en la migración interna, *In* Migración e integración en el Peru. H. F. Dobyns and M. C. Vasquez (eds.). Monografias Andinas Número 2. Lima, Peru pp. 184-187.

MISHKIN, BERNARD 1946 The contemporary Quechua. *In* Handbook of South American Indians. Volume 2. The Andean Civilizations. By Julian H. Steward (ed.), Smithsonian Institution, Bureau of American Ethnology, Bulletin 143, pp. 411-499.

MOORE, C. R. AND D. PRICE 1948 A study at high altitude of reproduction, growth, sexual maturity, and organ weights. J. Exp. Zool. 108: 171-216.

MURRA, J. V. 1968 An Aymara kingdom in 1567. Ethnohistory 15: 115-151.

NUÑEZ DEL PRADO, OSCAR 1955 Aspects of native Andean life. Kroeber Anthropological Society Papers, Number 12. pp. 1-21.

ROWE, JOHN HOWLAND 1946 Inca culture at the time of the Spanish conquest. *In* Handbook of South American Indians. Volume 2. The Andean civilizations. Julian H. Steward (ed.). Smithsonian Institution, Bureau of American Ethnology, Bulletin 143. pp. 411-499.

SOBREVILLA, L. A. 1967 Fertility at high altitude. Paper presented at PAHO/WHO/IBP Meeting of Investigators on Population Biology at Altitude, November 13-17. Washington, D.C.

——— 1971 Nacer en los Andes: Estudios fisiologicos sobre el embarazo y parto en la altura. Doctoral Thesis. Universidad Peruana Cayetano Heredia, Lima, Peru.

STYCOS, J. M. 1963 Culture and differential fertility in Peru. Population Studies 16: 257-270.

THOMAS, R. B. 1972 Human adaptation to energy flow in the high Andes. Ph.D. Thesis. The Pennsylvania State University, University Park, Pa.

WHITEHEAD, L. 1968 Altitude, fertility, and mortality in Andean countries. Population Studies 22: 335-346.

Interrelations Between Family Structure and Fertility in Yucatan

By James W. Ryder[1]

ABSTRACT

This paper presents data relevant to the resolution of the argument concerning the relations between extended family structure and fertility. A clarification of methodological and conceptual issues is attempted, and a new method for calculating births per year of exposure according to family structure is presented. A different direction for research concerning family structure, fertility and economics is briefly considered.

This paper presents data relevant to the resolution of the argument concerning the relations between extended[2] family structure and fertility. The relations between extended family structure and fertility have been treated most thoroughly by Lorimer (1954), Davis (1955), Davis and Blake (1956), Nag (1962, 1967) and Burch and Gendell (1970). Although specific differences exist in their discussions, especially with regard to level of analysis, the basic hypothesis states that high fertility is promoted by extended family structures through: 1. the encouragement of early and nearly universal marriage, 2. the reduction of the parents' costs of child bearing and child rearing through the availability of joint economic resources and additional personnel for child care, and 3. the motivation of both husband and wife to reproduce through inducements of increased status and potentially increased economical and political positions vis-à-vis other extended families.

In their critical evaluation of the literature dealing with the relations between extended family structure and fertility, Burch and Gendell (1970 p. 227) state: "There is a striking contrast between the wide acceptance of the proposition that the extended family encourages high fertility and the

---

[1]Institute of International Studies, University of California, Berkeley, 2234 Piedmont Avenue, Berkeley, California 94720.

[2]The terminological expression "extended family structure" will be used in this paper as an inclusive expression, subsuming various forms of extended family, including stem and lineal (e.g., patrilineal and fraternal extended families) families. It does not include joint family because members of extended families in Pencuyut and in Yucatan are not coparcerners, which is, I believe, the critical disjunction between the joint family and other forms of extended family structure.

scarcity of relevant empirical evidence." In an earlier study which summarized the relevant data and hypotheses concerning sociocultural factors
affecting fertility (as well as biological and environmental factors) Nag
(1962) used crosscultural data from nonindustrial societies to test several of
these hypotheses. Empirical data to test the effects of family structure on
fertility were not available, although the hypothesis was discussed in some
detail. In fact, recent empirical studies have not only failed to establish the
hypothesized relation between high fertility and extended family structure, but several have reported either no relation at all or the reverse
relation vis-à-vis nuclear families (e.g., Nag, 1967; Pakrasi and Malaker,
1967; Freedman et al. 1964; Liu, 1967).

The research upon which this paper is based was not restricted to the
relations between family structure and fertility, but dealt with a wide range
of sociocultural factors affecting fertility. The unit of analysis is the fertility
of individual women. An aggregate analysis at the societal level is rec-
ommended by Burch and Gendell as a necessary complement to individual analysis. However, comparable data on the level of fertility for entire
societies, classified as to whether the majority of women in the reproductive ages live in extended families or in nuclear families, is not available.
The data presented herein can contribute to filling that void, as well as
clarifying certain methodological and analytical issues. Although an
aggregate analysis cannot be made, eighteen months of field research in
Pencuyut has provided a broad range of in-depth data which furnish the
opportunity to use more exact definitions of family structure, residence
patterns and fertility measures. In addition, a better understanding of the
historical changes which have occurred in Pencuyut and in Yucatan has
been possible through the use of ethnohistorical studies and family re-
constitution. I decided to use the concept of the developmental cycle in
domestic groups and the role complexes of individuals, which vary
throughout the developmental cycle, in my analysis of demographic and
ethnographic data because the historical approach used in my field research resulted in a recognition of patterned change in the components of
households through time.

Thus, a family structure and postmarital residence patterns are defined
by several criteria including: 1. the relationship of individuals vis-à-vis the
head of the family or the head of the household, that is, in terms of descent
or affination; 2. the relationship between households, particularly with
regard to quality and quantity of interaction patterns; 3. spatial parameters,
specifically the arrangement of and authority over living and commensal
units; and 4. authority over the production and distribution of economic

resources. However, both family structure and postmarital residence patterns normally change one or more times during the life cycle of an individual. In other words, the composition of the domestic group changes cyclically, requiring role alterations among members in order to accommodate new forms of interaction. An obvious example of this can be seen in the status changes, and concommitant role alterations, of a newly married Pencuyuteño who brings his spouse into his father's household.

If the dynamic nature of family structure and postmarital residence patterns is understood, then the use of static typologies to define these processes is inappropriate. Moreover, this understanding leads directly to an evaluation of the different fertility measures used to compare the level of fertility in different family structures. For example, one of the most frequently used measures of fertility in such studies relates the cumulative fertility of all ever-married women to current family structure (or residence). In Pencuyut this measure, standardized for age, shows women living in nuclear families having 7.4 live births compared with 8.1 live births for women living in extended families. Another frequently used measure relates cumulative fertility to initial family structure (or residence). This measure (also age standardized) shows that women initially residing in a nuclear family in Pencuyut have a higher number of live births than women living in extended families: 8.6 and 7.6 respectively. Both measures, however, are totally unsatisfactory. The former presupposes either that women have lived in only one form of family structure, or that if a woman has lived in other family structures, her previous experience had no effect on her fertility. The latter measure presupposes that future experience will not alter fertility, which is related only to initial participation in one type of family structure. Neither supposition is defensible. A much more accurate method for calculating the level of fertility, as affected by family structure, is to attribute each birth to the form of family structure in which the mother resided at either the time of conception or parturition. This can be done in Pencuyut because the necessary questions, establishing duration and type of postmarital residence from marriage to the present, were asked during two censuses which I took, and have been checked against the birth registrations. In Pencuyut a small number of women have lived their entire lives in either nuclear or extended families, whereas the vast majority began their lives in extended families and moved to nuclear families. The first measure compares cumulative fertility of women aged 15-44, according to the amount of time spent in either extended or nuclear families, including shifts from one to the other. This measure parallels the Total Fertility Rate, although women are taken by single year of age from

15-44 instead of the usual seven five-year intervals from 15-49. The rate is calculated as the number of births per year of exposure.[3] This rate shows what level of fertility would be expected if a woman had the same age-specific fertility experienced by those women aged 15-44 presently living in Pencuyut. Women residing in extended families could expect 11.1 live births as compared to 8.9 live births for women living in nuclear families. If only those women who have lived in nuclear families or in extended families throughout their married lives are considered, there is an entirely different pattern. Women living in extended families could expect 10.6 live births compared with 10.7 live births for women living in nuclear families. Without controlling for family structure and using the number of births per year of exposure, women aged 44+ had an average of 10.7 live births. Despite small differences between observed levels of fertility based upon the number of births per woman as opposed to the number of births per year of exposure and despite the small N's involved, the rates help establish certain inconsistencies which require explanation. The first rate indicates that extended family structure does generate greater pressures which support higher levels of fertility than does nuclear family structure. The second rate indicates the reverse. That is, when the women who lived first in an extended family and later in a nuclear family are excluded from the population, even though their fertility has carefully been attributed to the family structure in which they were living at parturition, a dramatic change occurs in the rates.

The use of rates based upon exposure makes it possible to examine patterns of spacing by age and family structure. As noted previously, age at marriage has been stressed as an influential variable. In Pencuyut women who marry and reside in extended families follow the hypothesized pattern of marrying earlier than women who reside in nuclear families—19.1 in contrast to 20.0 years at marriage. If births are combined into three ten-year intervals (15-24, 25-34, 35-44) in order to make several gross comparisons, women residing in extended families have more children than women residing in nuclear families in all three age intervals. However, if women with transitional residence in different family structures are again excluded, the pattern is reversed, with the exception of the 35-44 age

$$3 \qquad \sum_{i=15}^{44} \frac{b_i}{Y_i}$$

where: b_i is the number of live births registered during the year, to mothers aged i in an interval of one year

y_i is the number of years of exposure of women of the same age group. These women who have transitional residence in different family structures (the majority of all cases) have one or two children in rapid succession in an extended family. They then move into a nuclear family where their fertility is higher than that of women wholly resident in an extended family, but lower than that of women wholly resident in a nuclear family.

Despite the advantages gained through refining specific conceptual and methodological problems, one obvious problem arises when family structure is viewed as a process rather than a type. Births can be attributed to different family structures[4] according to duration of residence in that particular family structure, but I am unaware of any quantitative method to measure the influence of the different family structures experienced during the life cycle of an individual. That is, if an individual is born and reared in an extended family for a number of years and then lives in a nuclear family until their marriage, are these early experiences unimportant in comparison with the different family structures in which they live upon marriage? It would be fallacious to suggest that if a woman followed the statistical norm in Pencuyut, living for several years in an extended family before moving into a nuclear family for the majority of her reproductive life, that her initial experiences did not influence her later behavior. These problems may not be as significant in extended families which form units within corporate unilineal descent groups, but within large scale agrarian societies, the category into which over half the world's population falls, corporate unilineal kin groups are unimportant.

The use of interaction patterns between families and households as a criterion to define family structure has created a second significant problem. Most nuclear families in Pencuyut i.e., those with households spatially separated from other households and who maintain control over their own production and the distribution of their economic resources, have interaction patterns which in quantity and intensity provide a number of characteristics which should promote high fertility, according to the hypothesis being examined. These households provide a source for additional economic assistance in case of emergency and make additional personnel available for child care. The status of both husband and wife are

[4]Although this conceptual and methodological refinement is new to the literature, it has an inherent contradiction. It requires breaking down the *process* of the developmental cycle, examining a segment of the cycle synchronically and then labelling that segment according to a predetermined classification or typology. The concept of the developmental cycle is thus violated in that it is a process wherein any given segment of that process is dynamically related to its antecedent and consequent forms.

increased with the birth of children. Moreover, both males and females stated clearly in interviews that they see their reproduction as potentially increasing their economic position, among other things. If this problem is frequently encountered, then no degree of refinement concerning collateral and generational extension to define family structure nor any improved measure of fertility is going to solve the dilemma. On the other hand, if the extended family fertility hypothesis ignores interaction patterns, it ignores data which could require a greatly revised hypothesis or could, in fact, make the distinction between extended and nuclear family structure meaningless with regard to their influence on fertility. This discussion has been based upon the assumption that the data being analyzed are relevant as tests of the extended family fertility hypothesis. However, Freedman (1961-62) has questioned whether modernization, especially with regard to the effects of declining mortality on family structure and fertility, may not have altered a causal link between family structure and fertility which had previously existed.

From an empiricist's point of view I would, therefore, recommend careful research along the lines specified by Burch and Gendell. However, from an historical or evolutionary perspective, the extended family fertility hypothesis appears superficial as an explanation for the present fertility differentials which do exist between developed and underdeveloped countries (cf. Polgar, 1972; Faris, 1973). It may be that fertility should be examined in relation to family structure only insofar as family structure is related to control over production and distribution of economic resources. Mamdani (1972) illustrates this with his detailed analysis of the failure of a birth control program in India's Punjab. Individual decisions concerning reproduction are based upon an analysis of the means by which survival can best be facilitated. Should the conclusion of such an analysis require a large number of children in order to work more land, enable some children to emigrate to urban areas to obtain wage labor and assure parents of their support and survival in old age, then a decision to have a large number of children will be made. Population dynamics, in this view, are seen as being directly affected by the economic conditions experienced by individuals who, themselves, determine what behavior is in their best interest rather than accepting advice concerning the value of small families based upon objectives formulated by government officials or a foreign research foundation. Moreover, these same policies, with regard to birth control, are in conflict with the fundamental nature of capitalist modes of production, which encourages or necessitates population growth among producers (Marx, 1967; Polgar, 1972; Hall, 1972; Faris, 1973). Therefore, since most populations of the world have been "affected by intimate economic relations with the 'outside' capitalist world" (Gunder Frank, 1966), the most reasonable points of departure in the study of the reasons for extant fertility levels in an underdeveloped area would be an understanding of that area's historical development and its relations to the larger economic units within which it operates (e.g., regional, national, international).

Received: 1 April 1975.

ACKNOWLEDGEMENT

I am grateful to Prithwis DasGupta for his help with the methodological sections of this paper. A debt of gratitude is due Edward Kurjack who ran all of the computer programs and gave critical advice throughout the various drafts of this paper. Rosemary Lee and William Petersen gave considerable critical assistance in improving the arguments found herein.

LITERATURE CITED

BURCH, THOMAS K. AND MURRAY GENDELL 1970 Extended family structure and fertility: some conceptual and methodological issues. Journal of Marriage and the Family **32:** 227-236.

DAVIS, KINGSLEY 1955 Institutional patterns favoring high fertility in underdeveloped areas. Eugenics Quarterly **2:** 33-39.

DAVIS, KINGSLEY AND JUDITH BLAKE 1956 Social structure and fertility: an analytic framework. Economic Development and Cultural Change **4:** 211-235.

FARIS, JAMES C. 1973 Social evolution, population, and production. Paper presented at the IXth International Congress of Anthropological and Ethnological Sciences, Chicago.

FREEDMAN, RONALD 1961-62 The sociology of human fertility: a trend report and bibliography. Current Sociology **10/11:** 35-119.

FREEDMAN, RONALD, JOHN Y. TAKESHITA AND T. H. SUN 1964 Fertility and family planning in Taiwan: a case study of demographic transition. American Journal of Sociology **70:** 16-27.

GUNDER FRANK, ANDRE 1966 The development of underdevelopment. Monthly Review. **18:** 17-30.

HALL, R. 1972 The demographic transition: stage four. Anthropology and population problems. Current Anthropology **13:** 203-278.

LIU, PAUL K. C. 1967 Differential fertility in Taiwan. Contributed Papers, Sydney Conference, International Union for the Scientific Study of Population; 363-370.

LORIMER, FRANK 1954 Culture and human fertility. UNESCO. Paris.

MAMDANI, M. 1972 The myth of population control. Monthly Review Press, New York.

MARX, K. 1967 Capital (3 volumes). International, New York.

NAG, MONI 1962   Factors affecting human fertility in non-industrial societies: a cross-cultural study. Yale University Publications in Anthropology 66.

————— 1967   Family type and fertility. Proceedings, World Population Conference, 1965. 2: 160-163. United Nations, New York.

PAKRASI, KANTI AND CHITTARANJAN MALAKER 1967   The relationship between family type and fertility. Milbank Memorial Fund Quarterly 45: 451-460.

POLGAR, S. 1972   Population history and population policies from an anthropological perspective. Anthropology and population problems. Current Anthropology 13: 203-278.

Symbiotic Relationship of High Fertility, High Childhood Mortality and Socio-Economic Status in an Urban Peruvian Population

By A. Roberto Frisancho,[1] Jane E. Klayman,[1] and Jorge Matos[2]

ABSTRACT

The reproductive, biological and socio-economic characteristics of a sample of 4,952 subjects derived from a Peruvian population of low and medium socio-economic status were studied. The study suggests that under conditions of poverty there exists a symbiotic relationship whereby low socio-economic status is associated with a less efficient mechanism to control family size. This characteristic permits the mother of low socio-economic status to attain a more complete child-bearing period. As childhood mortality is inversely related to socio-economic status, so, with an increase in childhood deaths there is an increase in live births in a compensatory fashion. High fertility is the net result of these interactions. The implications of these findings to attempts to decrease population fertility through birth control alone are discussed.

The demographic explosion that the developing countries are experiencing represents one of the most pressing problems of the present and future generations (Westoff, 1974). It is well known that this explosion is a product of the so-called "demographic transition" whereby rapid technological and social changes are reducing childhood mortality at a greater rate than fertility (Satin, 1969; Bogue, 1969; De Jong, 1972; Coale, 1974; Davis, 1974). Despite these facts, current programs for reducing the fertility of developing nations seem' to emphasize only the increased availability of birth control methods without regard to further socio-economic changes. However, because fertility in most non-Western populations is intimately bound to cultural factors and socio-economic characteristics (Demeny, 1974), such current programs of birth control have failed to have a major impact on fertility. Therefore, as a contribution to understanding the interrelationship between socio-economic factors and fertility we have investigated the reproductive characteristics of an urban Peruvian population of low socio-economic status.

[1]Center for Human Growth and Development and Department of Anthropology, The University of Michigan, Ann Arbor, Michigan 48104 U.S.A.
[2]Maternity Hospital of Lima, Peru.

METHODS AND MATERIALS

As part of a project concerned with human adaptation to environmental stress we investigated the reproductive, anthropometric, and socio-economic characteristics of an urban Peruvian population of low and medium socio-economic status. A total of 4,952 mothers and their corresponding newborns were studied. These subjects were studied in the Maternity Hospital of Lima (Maternidad de Lima) which primarily attends populations from poor socio-economic conditions. We chose this institution because it would permit us to obtain accurate information on reproductive characteristics. The data presented in this study correspond to 75% of the population attended during the months of July to December, 1973.

In the present study data on pregnancies, abortions, still births, live births, childhood mortality, per capita income, per capita expense on food, years of education and residency in Lima are examined. All this information was derived by a pediatrician and four obstetric nurses properly trained. Great care was taken to check the quality and validity of the information.

RESULTS AND DISCUSSION

As shown in Table 1, the population is generally characterized by a low socio-economic condition and the average length of schooling for the mothers was four years and for the fathers was six years. Furthermore, a majority of the families migrated from rural areas, and their average length of residence in Lima was 13 years (for both mother and father). The per capita income averaged $229, 63% of which was used for the purchase of food. Despite the young age of the mothers (average age of 25 years) the average number of live births per mother was 3.37 births. Of these about 9.5% died within the first five years, leaving 3.06 live offspring per mother.

Analysis of the reproductive and socio-economic characteristics of the mothers indicated that:

1. As illustrated in Figure 1 the Peruvian subjects age-for-age and especially after the age of 35 years have a greater number of live births per mother than the U.S. Whites. Furthermore, as shown in Figure 2, age at first live birth and subsequent live births occurs among the Peruvian subjects at an earlier age than in the U.S. Whites. This means that because women start reproducing at an earlier age and continue to reproduce through the late forties, they have a more complete child-bearing period when compared to the U.S. Whites. In order to test the possibility that there is a relationship between socio-economic status and the degree of

Table 1

Reproductive and Socio-economic Characteristics of an Urban Peruvian Population of Low Socio-economic Status Living in the City of Lima

	Mean	S.D.
Parental Information	(N = 4952)	
Age of Mother (Yrs)	24.84	6.16
Age of Father (Yrs)	29.91	7.61
Schooling of Mother (Yrs)	4.11	1.78
Schooling of Father (Yrs)	6.27	1.79
Per Capita Income ($)[1]	229.38	169.99
Per Capita Expense on Food($)[1]	144.62	68.05
Residency of Mother (Yrs)	13.72	6.51
Residency of Father (Yrs)	13.81	6.82
Number of Conceptions	3.65	2.81
Livebirths (N)	3.37	2.51
Childhood Mortality (%)	9.50	25.93
Live Offspring (N)	3.06	2.17

[1]Converted from Peruvian currency; $1.00 = 43.38 soles

Table 2

Regression Equation of best Predictors of live Births, as determined by Forward Stepwise Multiple Regression among a Peruvian Urban Population of Low Socio-economic Status

N	r	Regression Equation[1,2]
2299	0.82	$Y = -1.09 + 0.22$ (M. Age) $+ 1.14$ (Ch. Deaths) -0.0001 (Per Cap. Exp. Food) -0.00003 (Per Cap. Income) -0.04 (M. Schooling) S.E. 1.26

[1]Includes only the variables that obtained significance levels higher than 0.01. The order of appearance of the variables in the equation, irrespective of the value of the coefficient, indicates the order of importance in predicting live births.

[2]Non-significant variables were: mother's or father's length of residency in Lima, mother's civil status, father's years of schooling.

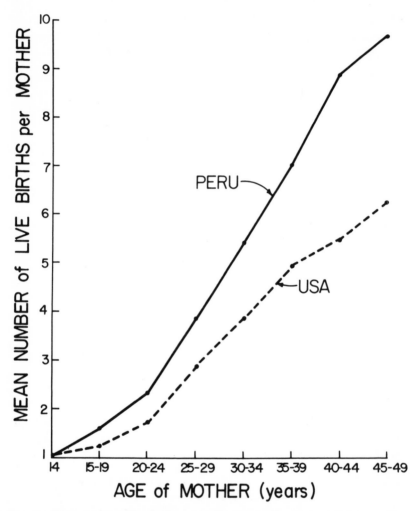

FIG. 1.   Mean number of live births per mother among Peruvian and U.S.A. mothers. Age-for-age and especially after the age of 30 years the Peruvian mothers have a significantly greater fertility than their U.S.A. counterparts.

completeness of the reproductive period, we have classified the Peruvian mothers into two socio-economic groups; above and below the per capita income of $229 and four years of schooling. Figure 3 shows that the less poor women in the hospital are predominantly below the age of 30 years while the women in the very poor group have a more complete age distri-

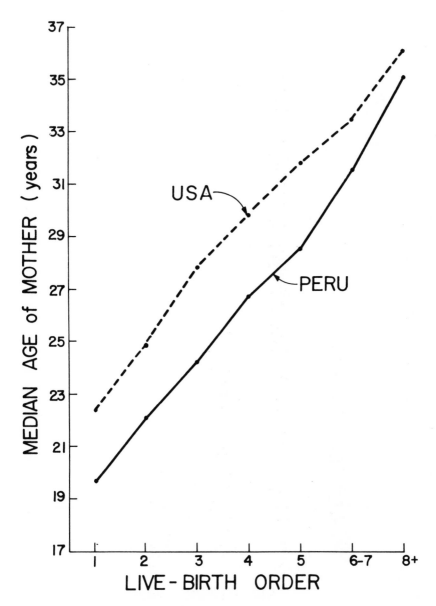

FIG. 2. Relationship between birth order and maternal age among Peruvian and U.S.A. mothers. First birth and subsequent births among the Peruvian mothers occur at a much earlier age than in the U.S.A.

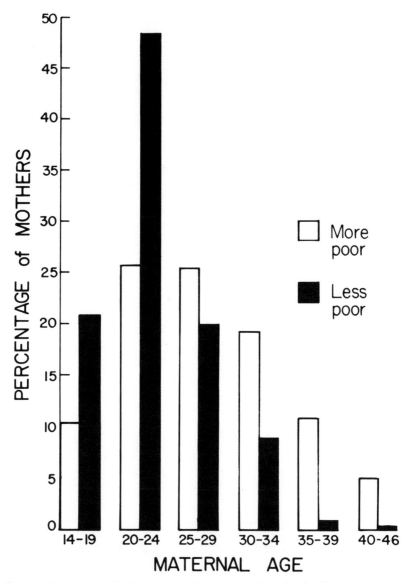

FIG. 3. Per cent age distribution among Peruvian mothers classified by socio-economic status. The less-poor mothers are predominantly below the age of 30 years while the women in the very poor group have a more complete age distribution.

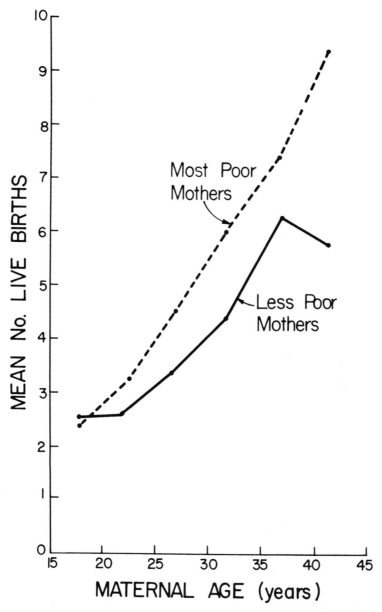

FIG. 4. Relationship between maternal age and mean number of live births among Peruvian mothers classified by socio-economic status. The most poor mothers at a given age and especially after the age of 30 years have a greater fertility than the less poor mothers.

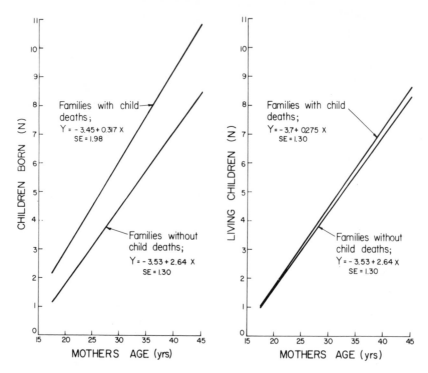

FIG. 5.   Influence of childhood deaths on live births and living children among Peruvian
mothers. Age-for-age among the mothers with no child deaths, the mean number of
live births is significantly lower than for those with child deaths. However, child
deaths do not appear to have a significant effect on mean number of living offspring.

bution. In other words, with a decrease in socio-economic status among
Peruvian mothers the child-bearing period is more complete. Furthermore, as shown in Figure 4, age-for-age and especially after the age of 30
years, the most poor mothers have a greater number of live births than
their less poor counterparts.

2. As shown in Table 2, after maternal age, the best predictor of live
births is the total number of childhood deaths. The third, fourth, and fifth
predictors include per capita expense on food, per capita income and education of mother. The fact that there is a positive relationship between live
births and childhood deaths would suggest that in this population there is
a compensatory mechanism whereby high childhood deaths are compensated for by high live births.

A test of this hypothesis can be seen in Figure 5. As shown by these data the number of live births age-for-age among the mothers who had no childhood deaths is much lower than that of the mothers who had more than one child death. However, between the mothers with and without childhood deaths the number of children alive is quite similar. Taking together these data it would appear that in this population one important factor contributing to variations in live births is childhood mortality. A recent study of an Indian sample has also found that high childhood mortality is associated with high fertility and vice versa (Singh, 1974).

Studies among Australian aborigines indicate that high fertility is a response to high mortality (Jones, 1970; Yengoyan, 1972). These studies suggested that the Australian populations were aware of high childhood death rates, and one of their responses was to maintain high fertility to

POVERTY and FERTILITY

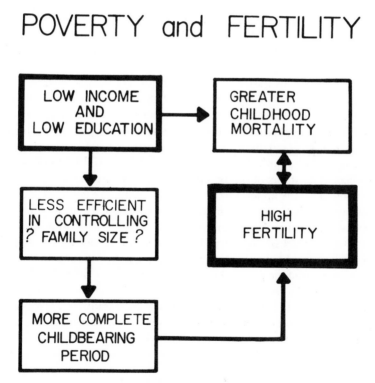

FIG. 6.   Schematic representation of the symbiotic relationship between socio-economic and biological factors leading to high fertility under conditions of poverty.

counterbalance the inevitable deaths which were and still are commonplace. Thus it would appear that the existence of a close relationship between fertility and childhood mortality is not population specific, and may occur as long as the population is subjected to conditions leading to high childhood mortality. In other words, high infant mortality is not only the fact in such societies, but also the expectation. Furthermore, among non-Western impoverished populations there is a lack of governmental care for the aged, and high fertility may be considered one means of ensuring one's life during old age. Therefore, high fertility under poor socio-economic conditions leading to high childhood mortality has obvious survival value both in short and long-term perspectives.

As schematized in Figure 6, under conditions of poverty there appears to be a symbiotic relationship whereby low socio-economic status by whatever sociologic or behavioral means is associated with a less efficient mechanism to control family size. This characteristic permits the mother of low socio-economic status to attain a more complete child-bearing period, which in turn results in high fertility. As childhood mortality is inversely related to socio-economic status, with an increase in childhood deaths there is an increase in live births in a compensatory fashion. The net result of these interactions under conditions of poverty is high fertility.

The present study demonstrates that there is a relationship between fertility, childhood mortality, socio-economic status and completeness of the child-bearing period. These findings suggest that attempts to decrease fertility among populations of low socio-economic status must include a program whereby both the availability of birth control methods and the socio-economic status of the population must be improved. The fact that childhood mortality appears to be one of the major predictors of live births would suggest that a mechanism to decrease childhood mortality should be of prime importance. In other words, the fertility level of a population cannot be changed simply through birth control methods. Such a change can only be brought about with accompanying improvements in the socio-economic status of the population which in turn reduce the toll of childhood mortality and decrease the child-bearing period of the mother. Since childhood mortality is a function of socio-economic status, any program that improves the socio-economic status of a population will result in decreasing childhood mortality and hence have positive effects in reducing fertility.

ACKNOWLEDGMENTS

This study was supported in part by grant GS-37542 X of the National Science Foundation and by research funds of the University of Michigan.

The authors wish to thank the mothers who participated in this study and the staff of the Maternity Hospital of Lima, Peru, without whom this study would not have been possible. We gratefully acknowledge the assistance of Miss Anne Spiceland, and Mr. Robert Wainwright for their assistance in the preparation of this manuscript.

Received: 25 February 1975.

LITERATURE CITED

BOGUE, D. J.   1969   Principles of demography. Wiley, New York.

COALE, A. J.   1974   The history of the human population. Sci. Amer. **231:** 40-51.

DAVIS, K.   1974   The immigrations of human populations. Sci. Amer. **231:** 92-105.

DE JONG, G. F.   1972   Patterns of human fertility and mortality. *In* The Structure of human populations. Harrison, G. A. and A. J. Boyce, eds. Clarendon Press, Oxford.

DEMENY, P.   1974   The populations of the underdeveloped countries. Sci. Amer. **231:** 148-159.

JONES, F. L.   1970   The Aboriginal population of Australia: Present distribution and probable future growth. Canberra.

SATIN, M. S.   1969   An empirical test of the descriptive validity of the theory of demographic transition on a fifty-three nation sample. Sociol. Q. **10:** 190-203.

SINGH, K. P.   1974   Child mortality, social status, and fertility in India. Soc. Biol. **21:** 385-388.

WESTOFF, C. F.   1974   The populations of the developed countries. Sci. Amer. **231:** 108-120.

YENGOYAN, A. A.   1972   Biological and demographic components in aboriginal Australian socio-economic organization. Oceania, **43:** 85-95.

Fertility and other Demographic Aspects of the Canadian Eskimo Communities of Igloolik and Hall Beach

By Phyllis J. McAlpine[1,2] and Nancy E. Simpson[1]

ABSTRACT

The reproductive histories of 89 mothers in Igloolik and 43 in Hall Beach, two neighboring Canadian Eskimo communities in the eastern Canadian Arctic were compared according to the mothers' reproductive status. A total of 945 fetuses, consisting of 826 (87.4%) livebirths, 28 (3.0%) stillbirths, 90 (9.5%) spontaneous abortions and one (0.1%) unknown outcome were reported. Approximately 25% of all livebirths died before 15 years of age. On the average, premenopausal mothers in Hall Beach experienced menarche about 11 months earlier and had their first baby about 12 months earlier than did their counterparts in Igloolik. The natural reproductive period ranged from 28 to 43 years with the mean age of menopause at 52 years. The average family size per naturally postreproductive female was 11.1 ± 0.9 livebirths plus stillbirths for the two communities combined. Premenopausal women had another child sooner when their previous birth died at less than one year than when it lived longer. If the previous birth lived for more than one year, premenopausal mothers had a subsequent child about 4 months sooner after male than after female births. No patterns of child spacing were found in the records of naturally postreproductive women. Birth rates in Igloolik and Hall Beach were 51.4 and 36.3 per thousand, respectively. 11.7 sets of multiple births per thousand births were reported. The average birth weight was 3.12 kg. Caucasian admixture, as calculated from pedigree analysis, was estimated to be about 3% in both communities. The coefficient of inbreeding in Igloolik was estimated to be about 0.001; no consanguineous matings were reported in Hall Beach.

The changing reproductive histories and the extent of racial admixture and inbreeding have been studied in two closely related Eskimo communities in the eastern Canadian Arctic: (Fig. 1) Igloolik (69°N, 82°W) and Hall Beach (69°N, 81°W). This study documents fertility and population structure of these communities at a time when the industrialized "Western civilization" has begun to have a profound and rapid effect on the lifestyle of the Eskimos. It is hoped that the data may be used for comparisons with other Eskimo populations and with the same populations in the future at a time when "aculturalization" is complete. The collection of these data

[1]Departments of Paediatrics and Biology, Queen's University, Kingston, Ontario, Canada.

[2]Present Address: Division of Genetics, (Department of Paediatrics and Department of Anatomy) University of Manitoba, and Health Sciences Children's Centre, Winnipeg, Manitoba, Canada.

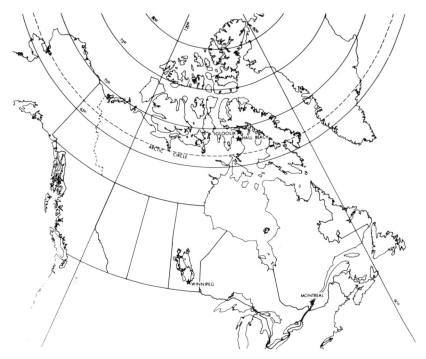

FIG. 1.   Map of Canada showing geographical location of Igloolik and Hall Beach (adapted from McAlpine et al. 1974).

formed part of the Canadian contribution to the Human Adaptability Section of the International Biological Programme's multidisciplinary investigation of the biological basis of these Eskimos' successful adaptation to life in their Arctic environment. A related aspect of this study, the description of the population of Igloolik with respect to genetic markers in blood, has been already reported (McAlpine et al. 1974).

DESCRIPTION OF THE COMMUNITIES

The Igloolik and Hall Beach Eskimos originally lived in isolated camps, each composed of a few families, scattered throughout the vicinity of the present-day communities in the Foxe Basin. At that time, their lifestyle was traditional and centered around hunting, fishing, and trapping. Although contact between neighboring Eskimo groups was quite common, contact with non-Eskimos probably has occurred only within the last 200 years and, until recently, was limited to occasional visits by traders, whalers, explorers, and missionaries. During the 1940's the Canadian Government initiated a program to encourage the Eskimos to move into the newly established communities of Igloolik and Hall Beach. Over the following thirty years, the Eskimos in the area gradually took up permanent residence in the settlements and at the time of the study only one family remained year round in a camp; this was in the Hall Beach area.

Since their "urbanization" the number of Eskimo families adhering to a "quasi-traditional" lifestyle has been decreasing. Some families live entirely on their incomes from providing services to the communities, or from social assistance, or as is the case in Hall Beach, by working at a nearby radar installation. Many families combine salaried employment with hunting and trapping and, thus, live partly in a traditional manner and partly in a contemporary manner. The isolation of the original settlements is decreasing and at the time of this study, approximately 35-40 non-Eskimos (about 7%) were living in Igloolik and approximately 20 (about 7%) in Hall Beach.

METHODS

During two field expeditions, personal interviews were held with the adult Eskimo residents of Igloolik (January 1971) and Hall Beach (October 1971) at which time they were questioned as to the identity of their first degree relatives, i.e., parents, sibs, and children. The information obtained was substantiated and supplemented with recorded vital statistics and data collected from various field expeditions (1969-71). Pedigrees were constructed to demonstrate the biological relationships of the persons interviewed and these relationships, together with the vital statistics information were analysed by computer for a number of demographic features. Reference to the sociological aspects of the population structure will be made only as they affect the biological aspects.

The data presented here relate to all Igloolik and Hall Beach mothers interviewed in 1971 and to their families. All of the females interviewed who were known to have experienced at least one pregnancy were classified from their medical histories (Hildes and Schaefer, personal communication) according to their present reproductive status as (1) premenopausal or (2) postreproductive. The postreproductive groups were subdivided into a) artificially postreproductive, i.e. those who had had their postreproductive state induced by surgery (e.g. tubal ligation, hysterectomy) or by known disorders of the reproductive tract (e.g.

Sheehan's syndrome) which prevented them from having further children, and b) naturally postreproductive, i.e. those in whom the menopause had occurred naturally.

As the abortion data were collected by interview, it has not been possible to eliminate the uncertainty of gestational age of the "aborted fetuses." As far as is known all abortions were spontaneous.

Infant and childhood deaths include all deaths known to have occurred at age 14 years or less. When death records were not available, the information was obtained at interview. In some instances the interviewees were able to provide the age at death; in a considerable number of instances the age at death of these children was not known and they were described as having "died young." In the event that some of the older children were post-pubertal, none were known to have had any children. Thus, none of these persons contributed to the gene pool of the next generation.

The mean birth weights were calculated using the data from all births for which birth weight was available. All of these births had taken place in the local nursing stations or in hospitals where balances were available for weighing the babies at the time of birth. There were not sufficient numbers of premature births recorded to compare birth weights by length of gestation.

RESULTS

Present Population: Size and Sex Ratio

The distributions of the populations by age and sex for the two villages are presented in Figures 2 and 3.

There were 564 Eskimos (300 males; 264 females) living in Igloolik as of January, 1971 and 248 (125 males; 123 females) in Hall Beach as of October, 1971. In Igloolik the sex ratio (males:females) was 1.14 while in Hall Beach it was 1.02. In both villages the age range was from newborn to 74 years. A high proportion of the residents of both villages were young persons as reflected by the median age groups: 10-14 years for both males and females in Igloolik and for females in Hall Beach, and 15-19 years for males in Hall Beach. In Igloolik 18 out of 300 (6.0%) of the females and 15 out of 264 (5.7%) of the males were 50 years of age or older; in Hall Beach 8 out of 125 (6.4%) of the males and 3 out of 125 (2.4%) of the females were at least 50 years of age.

Reproductive Histories

Fertile Females. In Igloolik 14 out of 23 females (60.9%) who were 20-24 years of age and three out of 24 females (12.5%) who were 15-19 years of age

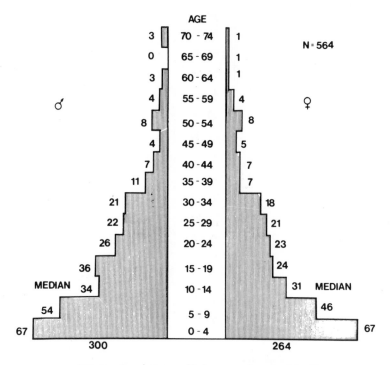

Fig. 2. Population profile by age and sex for Igloolik.

had had at least one child. In Hall Beach 11 out of 12 females (91.7%) who were 20-24 years of age and five out of 15 females (33.3%) who were 15-19 years of age had had at least one child. The remaining females in the 15-19 and 20-24 year age groups in the two communities who had not had any children were single or had been married for less than one year, and thus can not be considered infertile yet. Except for one 34-year-old woman in Igloolik who has been married for some time and possibly is infertile, all other women 25 years of age or older in the two communities had experienced at least one pregnancy.

Of the 89 mothers in Igloolik, 72 (80.9%) were classified as premenopausal, 6 (6.7%) as artificially postreproductive and 11 (12.4%) as naturally postreproductive. In Hall Beach 35 (81.4%) of the 43 mothers were premenopausal, 4 (9.3%) were artificially postreproductive and 4 (9.3%) were naturally postreproductive. The distributions of mothers amongst the reproductive classes were similar in the two communities.

Age at menarche and at birth of first child. Mean ages at menarch and at the birth of the first child were calculated from the available data

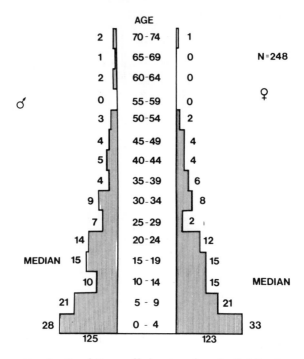

FIG. 3.   Population profile by age and sex for Hall Beach.

according to the mothers' village of residence and reproductive category (Table 1). On the average, menarche occurred at an earlier age in Hall Beach premenopausal mothers (13.4 ± 0.2 yr) than in Igloolik pre-menopausal mothers (14.3 ± 0.2 yr) (t = 2.394, p<.05). In addition, this same group of Hall Beach mothers had their first baby at an earlier age (16.9 ± 0.3 yr) than did their counterparts in Igloolik (17.9 ± 0.3 yr) (t = 2.554, p<.025).

   Age at menopause and duration of reproductive period. The mean age at menopause was 52.3 ± 1.0 yr for the 11 naturally postreproductive women in Igloolik for whom data were available and 49.3 ± 1.7 yr for the four naturally postreproductive women in Hall Beach. As the difference between these means was not statistically significant, the two groups were combined. The mean age at menopause was 51.5 ± 0.9 yr for all naturally postreproductive mothers. The period from menarche to natural menopause ranged from 28 to 43 years with a mean of 36.3 ± 1.9 yr for the eight Igloolik mothers for whom these data were available. For the four

Table 1

Mean Age at Menarche and at the Birth of the First Child according to Mother's Village of Residence and Reproductive Category

Village of residence	Mothers' Reproductive category	Number of mothers	Mean age (yr) ± SE at menarche*	Number of mothers	Mean age (yr) ± SE at birth of first child
Igloolik	Premenopausal	62	14.3 ± 0.2	52	17.9 ± 0.3
	Postreproductive				
	Artificially	5	14.0 ± 0.4	4	17.8 ± 0.6
	Naturally	8	15.1 ± 0.9	4	17.0 ± 0.9
Hall Beach	Premenopausal	31	13.4 ± 0.2	29	16.9 ± 0.2
	Postreproductive				
	Artificially	4	13.5 ± 0.3	2	18.5 ± 4.5
	Naturally	4	13.5 ± 0.3	1	19.0 ± 0.0

*Hildes and Schaefer, personal communication.

Table 2

Number of Fetuses and Outcome of Delivery by Mothers' Village of Residence, and Reproductive Category

Village of residence	Mothers' Reproductive category	Number of mothers		Number and percent*								Total
				Livebirths		Stillbirths		Abortions		Unknown		
		N	%	N	%	N	%	N	%	N	%	N
Igloolik	Premenopausal	72	(80.9)	427	(89.1)	14	(2.9)	37	(7.7)	1	(0.2)	479
	Postreproductive											
	Artificially	6	(6.7)	20	(71.4)	1	(3.6)	7	(25.0)	—	—	28
	Naturally	11	(12.4)	110	(91.7)	6	(5.0)	4	(3.3)	—	—	120
	Total	89	(100.0)	557	(88.8)	21	(3.4)	48	(7.7)	1	(0.2)	627
Hall Beach	Premenopausal	35	(81.4)	180	(83.7)	4	(1.9)	31	(14.4)	—	—	215
	Postreproductive											
	Artificially	4	(9.3)	39	(79.6)	3	(6.1)	7	(14.3)	—	—	49
	Naturally	4	(9.3)	50	(92.6)	—	—	4	(7.4)	—	—	54
	Total	43	(100.0)	269	(84.6)	7	(2.2)	42	(13.2)	—	—	318
Combined	Grand Total	132	(100.0)	826	(87.4)	28	(3.0)	90	(9.5)	1	(0.1)	945

*Percent of all births

Hall Beach mothers for whom data were available, this period ranged from 33 to 41 years with a mean of 35.8 ± 1.8 years. The mean of the pooled data was 36.0 ± 1.3 yr.

Number of fetuses. The number of fetuses and the outcome of each delivery were tabulated according to the village of residence and the reproductive category of the mothers at the time of this survey (Table 2). The 89 women in Igloolik who had experienced at least one pregnancy reported 557 livebirths, 21 stillbirths, and 48 abortions. It was not possible to determine whether the outcome of one additional pregnancy was a

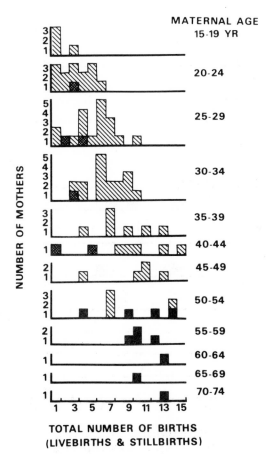

FIG. 4.   Distribution of the numbers of livebirths plus stillbirths by mothers' reproductive category and age for Igloolik.

livebirth or stillbirth. The 43 women in Hall Beach who had been gravid at least once reported 269 livebirths, seven stillbirths and 42 abortions. The distribution of livebirths and stillbirths did not differ with the mothers' reproductive class or her village of residence. Similar comparisons for abortions could not be made because of the uncertainty of the gestational ages and of the numbers of abortions.

The numbers of livebirths plus stillbirths (family size) plotted according to the reproductive category and maternal age group are presented in Figures 4 and 5. Family size ranged from one to 15 births for the 89 females

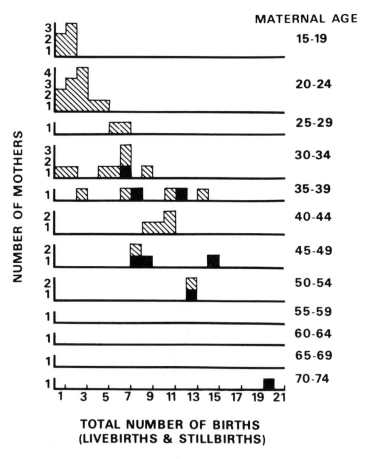

FIG. 5.   Distribution of the numbers of livebirths plus stillbirths by mothers' reproductive category and age for Hall Beach.

Table 3

Mean Number of Livebirths plus Stillbirths per Postreproductive Woman who had Partuated, according to Mothers' Village of Residence and Reproductive Category

Village of residence	Mothers' Postreproductive category	Number of mothers	Mean number of Livebirths & Stillbirths ± SE
Igloolik	Artificial	6	3.5 ± 0.8
	Natural	11	10.5 ± 0.8
	All postreproductive	17	5.3 ± 0.6
Hall Beach	Artificial	4	10.5 ± 1.8
	Natural	4	12.5 ± 2.7
	All postreproductive	8	11.5 ± 1.6
Combined	All Natural	15	11.1 ± 0.9

in Igloolik who had been gravid at least once and from one to 20 births for the 43 Hall Beach females who had been gravid at least once. Amongst women who had completed their families the 11 naturally postreproductive women in Igloolik reported a mean of 10.5 ± 0.8 children while the corresponding group of four mothers in Hall Beach reported a mean of 12.5 ± 2.7 children (Table 3). The six women in Igloolik in whom sterility had been induced reported an average of 3.5 ± 0.8 children, which was significantly less than the mean of 10.5 ± 1.8 reported by the corresponding group in Hall Beach (t = 4.010, p<.005).

Infant and childhood mortality. The tabulation of infant/childhood deaths by mothers' village of residence and reproductive category is presented in Table 4. At least 109 children (44 ♂ : 46 ♀ : 19 sex unknown) of the 557 (19.6%) liveborn children of Iglooik mothers died as babies or as children and 63 children (39 ♂ : 20 ♀ : 4 sex unknown) of the 269 (23.4%) liveborn children of the Hall Beach mothers died in infancy or childhood.

The Hall Beach premenopausal mothers reported fewer infant/childhood deaths (17.8%) than did the women in this community who were artificially postreproductive (35.9%) (χ^2 = 5.30, df 1, 0.025>p>0.010) or naturally postreproductive (34.0%) (χ^2 = 5.21, df 1, 0.025>p>0.010). No such intracommunity differences were found in the Igloolik data. When each reproductive class was compared for the two communities, there were no differences.

Table 4

A Comparison of Infant/Childhood Mortality of Liveborn Children by Mothers' Village of Residence and Reproductive Category

Village of Residence	Mothers' Reproductive category	Number of Livebirths	Infant/childhood deaths	
			Number of deaths	% of livebirths
Igloolik	Premenopausal	427	78	18.3
	Postreproductive			
	Artificially	20	7	35.0
	Naturally	110	24	21.8
	Total	557	109	19.6
Hall Beach	Premenopausal	180	32	17.8
	Postreproductive			
	Artificially	39	14	35.9
	Naturally	50	17	34.0
	Total	269	63	23.4

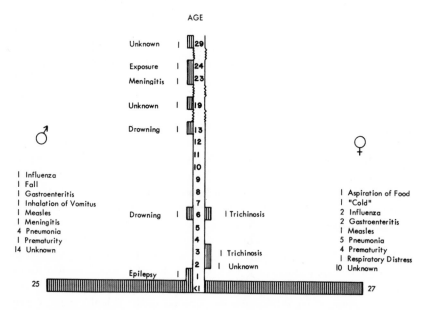

FIG. 6.   Distribution by sex, age, and cause of death of 62 children among 557 livebirths of 89 Igloolik mothers.

The distribution of deaths by age for the two communities from death records only (Figs. 6 and 7; Table 4 includes deaths reported at interview) further illustrates the very high infant mortality rate in the two communities; 52 out of 62 recorded deaths (83.9%) from Igloolik and 17 out of the 29 (58.6%) in Hall Beach indicated that the age at death was one year or less.

Sex ratios. The sex distribution of children at birth (livebirths and stillbirths) and of those dying in infancy or childhood, together with the sex ratios tabulated according to mother's village and reproductive category are presented in Table 5. Comparisons of the sex ratios between the different groups of children for each of the mothers' reproductive categories in each of the villages revealed no statistically significant differences.

Child spacing. The interval in months from the time of each livebirth (to be called the index birth) until the outcome of the next successive pregnancy was calculated according to the outcome of the index birth in terms of the village of residence and the reproductive category of the mothers interviewed (Table 6). As the differences in mean intervals for corre-

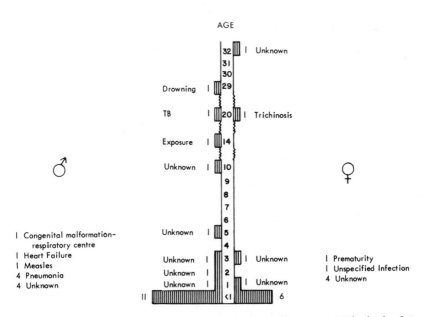

Fig. 7.   Distribution by sex, age, and cause of death of 29 children among 269 livebirths of 43 Hall Beach mothers.

Table 5

Distribution of Fetuses by Sex with Sex Ratios at Birth and of Infant/Childhood Deaths according to Mothers' Village of Residence and Reproductive Category

Village of residence	Mothers' Reproductive category	Number of					Number of Infant/Childhood deaths	Infant/Childhood deaths' sex ratio
		Sex	Livebirths	Stillbirths	Sex ratio at birth			
Igloolik	Premenopausal	M	218	2 ⎱	1.08	35 ⎱		1.00
		F	197	7 ⎰		35 ⎰		
		UK	12	5		8		
	Postreproductive Artificially	M	7	— ⎱	0.70	1 ⎱		0.33
		F	10	— ⎰		3 ⎰		
		UK	3	1		3		
	Naturally	M	54	2 ⎱	1.22	8 ⎱		1.00
		F	46	— ⎰		8 ⎰		
		UK	10	4		8		

Mothers'			Number of					
Village of residence	Reproductive category	Sex	Livebirths	Stillbirths	Sex ratio at birth	Number of Infant/Childhood deaths		Infant/Childhood deaths' sex ratio
Hall Beach	Premenopausal	M	93	1 ⎫	1.08	16 ⎫		1.23
		F	85	2 ⎬		13 ⎬		
		UK	2	1		3		
	Postreproductive Artificially	M	22	3 ⎫	1.56	10 ⎫		3.33
		F	16	— ⎬		3 ⎬		
		UK	1	—		1		
	Naturally	M	26	— ⎫	1.08	13 ⎫		3.25
		F	24	— ⎬		4 ⎬		
		UK	—	—		—		

*M = Male, F = Female, UK = Sex unknown.

Table 6

Child Spacing in Igloolik and Hall Beach

Reproductive category of mother	Outcome of index birth		Number	Interval in months ± SE from time of each livebirth until outcome of successive pregnancy
	Sex*	Survival		
Premenopausal	M	>1 year	156	25.9 ± 0.9
	F	>1 year	134	29.4 ± 1.3
	M	<1 year	22	19.8 ± 1.4
	F	<1 year	15	19.3 ± 1.6
	M or F	<1 year	37	19.6 ± 1.1
Postreproductive				
Naturally	M	>1 year	28	36.6 ± 3.4
	F	>1 year	20	31.0 ± 1.4
	M or F	<1 year	5	25.3 ± 4.6

*M = Male, F = Female.

sponding categories were not statistically significant when inter-community comparisons were made, the data for Igloolik and Hall Beach were pooled. For premenopausal mothers, the mean interval after a livebirth who lived for more than one year, until the outcome of the next successive pregnancy was found to be shorter when the index birth was a male (mean: 25.9 ± 0.9 months) than when it was a female (mean: 29.4 ± 1.3 months) (t = 2.206, p<.05). The differences between the means of the corresponding intervals of 36.6 ± 3.4 months after the birth of a male and of 31.0 ± 1.4 months after the birth of a female to postreproductive (naturally) females were not statistically significant. If the index birth lived for more than a year, the interval until the successive birth to naturally postreproductive mothers was significantly longer than that to premenopausal mothers, when the index child was male (36.6 ± 3.4 v. 25.9 ± 0.9 months, t = 4.075, p<0.001), but not when the index child was a female (31.0 ± 1.4 v. 29.4 ± 1.3 months).

If the index birth of a premenopausal mother lived for less than a year, these women had another child sooner than when the first child lived, whether the first of the pair was a male (19.8 ± 1.4 v. 25.9 ± 0.9 months, t = 2.381, p<.05) or a female (19.3 ± 1.6 v. 29.4 ± 1.3 months, t = 2.535, p<.025). As no sex difference was found between the mean intervals following index births who lived less than one year (19.8 ± 1.4 months for males and 19.3± 1.6 months for females) who were born to premenopausal women, the intervals for both sexes were combined to give a mean of 19.6± 1.1 months. This mean was not statistically different from the mean of the corresponding interval (25.3 ± 4.6 months) for naturally postreproductive mothers. Although premenopausal mothers on the average had another child sooner when the index birth died at less than one year as compared to when it lived for more than one year, such a difference could not be demonstrated for naturally postreproductive mothers between the case when the index birth died at less than one year and after a surviving male (25.3± 4.6 months v. 36.6± 3.4 months) or a female (25.3± 4.6 v. 31.0± 1.4 months). No statistically significant difference was found between the mean intervals following an index birth who lived for less than one year when the data for premenopausal (19.6 ± 1.1 months) and naturally postreproductive women (25.3 ± 4.6 months) were compared.

Birth rate. In the calendar year preceding the collection of demographic data in each community, 29 children were born to Igloolik mothers corresponding to a birth rate of 51.4 per thousand population while nine children were born to Hall Beach mothers during the same period, corresponding to a birth rate of 36.3 per thousand population.

Multiple births. One set of female quadruplets, two pairs of male, three pairs of unlike sex twins and one pair of unknown sex twins were born to mothers living in Igloolik. Three of the quadruplets and the twins of unknown sex were stillborn; the remaining multiple birth infants were liveborn. Two pairs of female, and one pair of unlike sex twins were born to Hall Beach mothers. All were livebirths. The frequency of sets of multiple births was 12.1 per thousand (7 out of 578) births (livebirths and stillbirths) in Igloolik and 10.9 per thousand (3 out of 276) births in Hall Beach. The difference between the two communities was not statistically significant and the data were combined to give an overall frequency of 11.7 sets of multiple births per thousand births.

Birth weights. The birth weights of only a limited number of children born to Igloolik and Hall Beach mothers were available. As no statistically significant sex difference nor difference between the two communities in the mean birth weights was found, the birth weights were pooled to give a mean birth weight of 3.12 ± .04 kg (sample size: 164).
size: 164).

Caucasian Admixture

From the information obtained from family interviews in Igloolik, seven individuals claimed to have had one Caucasian parent, 12 to have had a Caucasian grandparent and seven to have had a Caucasian greatgrandparent. At the time of the study, the total population of Igloolik was 564 individuals and thus 1.31% of the genes of the total population would be expected to be Caucasian in origin. In addition, three persons were suspected from the interview data to have had a Caucasian parent, 28 to have had a Caucasian grandparent and 16 to have had a Caucasian great-grandparent and consquently an additional 1.87% of the genes in the Igloolik gene pool may be Caucasian in origin. When the estimates from the documented and the undocumented family histories are combined, 3.17% of the genes in the Igloolik gene pool may be Caucasian in origin. Data obtained from genetic markers in blood studies indicated that $7.6 \pm 1.0\%$ of the genes in the Igloolik gene pool were expected to be Caucasian in origin when the immunoglobin $Gm^{3,5,13,14}$ haplotype, the P^c allele of red cell acid phosphatase and the PGD^c allele of 6-phosphogluconate de-hydrogenase were used for calculations. If the $Gm^{1,2,21}$ haplotype also is considered to be Caucasoid, then $7.3 \pm 1.0\%$ of the Igloolik gene pool may be Caucasoid (McAlpine et al. 1974).

In Hall Beach, two individuals claimed to have had a Caucasian parent, 26 to have a Caucasian grandparent and 18 to have had a Caucasian greatgrandparent and thus at least 3.93% of the genes in the Hall Beach pool may be Caucasian in origin. Genetic markers were not examined in this population and hence an estimate could not be made from marker data.

Coefficient of Inbreeding

Eight of the 98 (8.2%) marriages in Igloolik with at least one spouse alive at the time of this survey were known to be or to have been consanguine-ous. From the nature of the genetic relationships of their ancestors, the present day Igloolik population has been estimated according to the method outlined by Stern (1960), to have an inbreeding coefficient of at least 0.001 (Table 7). This estimate has been derived from the data for the persons alive in Igloolik at the time of the study and includes only those couples who had at least one living child. None of the Hall Beach couples were known to be consanguineous.

DISCUSSION

Demographic data for the Eskimo villages of Igloolik and Hall Beach have been presented here in order to provide base line data of the re-productive histories, Caucasian admixture and inbreeding in these two communities for future restudies and for comparisons with similar data on other Eskimos. It must be borne in mind that prior to the 1940's no vital

Table 7

Inbreeding in the Igloolik Population

Relationship of parents	Coefficient of inbreeding (F) of offspring	Number of couples	Number of offspring	
			living in Igloolik	dead
First cousins	1/16	1	4	3
Half first cousins	1/32	2	17	4
Half first cousins, once removed	1/64	2	10	3
First cousins, once removed	1/32	1	1	1+ several abortions
First cousins, parents of one spouse half first cousins, parents of other spouse half first cousins, once removed	[1/16 (1+1/32+1/64)]	1	—	—
Second cousins, parents of one spouse half first cousins	[1/64 (1+1/32)]	1	—	—

Coefficient of inbreeding of persons living in Igloolik: 0.0010.
Incidence of consanguineous marriages: 8/98 = 0.082.

statistics records of the Eskimos were kept, and even after they were initiated, the reporting of information from people still living in camps was not always complete. The data concerning the persons who were born and died before the 1940's have been based only on information obtained during the personal interviews and thus are subject to the fallibilities of human recollection. Because deaths may be unhappy occurrences, families may tend to put these events out of their minds, particularly if the deceased were babies or children. It is quite likely, therefore, that the infant mortality data and, hence, the total number of births reported are underestimates of the actual numbers. Furthermore, the widespread Eskimo custom of adopting children between families may have affected some of the reporting of biological relationships. It is only recently that adoptions have been recorded by the judiciary and, thus, in former times confusion over the identity of an individual's biological relatives was possible. Despite the ommissions which may exist in the data, we feel that the information we have collected does describe as well as possible the present demography including reproductive histories of these two very rapidly changing communities.

Although there has been long-standing continuing migration of Eskimos back and forth between Igloolik and Hall Beach resulting in a close relationship between the two communities, some differences in the demography of the two communities have been detected.

The rise in the total population of Igloolik from 102 persons in 1941 to 552 persons in 1964 probably reflects the movement of greater numbers of families from camps in the area into the permanent settlement (Figure 8). Since 1964, the population has remained relatively constant at about 550 persons except for a drop to 486 in 1966 (Statistics Canada 1941, 1951, 1956, 1961, 1966, and 1971). In 1966-67 there was a widespread outbreak of mumps and influenza in the community and as a result a number of persons died while others migrated out of the community. Data are not available to determine whether or not these events had a differential sex effect which could be reflected in the sex ratio in Igloolik at the time of this study.

In Igloolik and Hall Beach it appears that all Eskimos of childbearing age marry and, if they are fertile, which they usually are, they have offspring. In the traditional Eskimo life a couple was an economic and social unit; a man needed a wife to care for the skins from the animals that he hunted, to make clothing, to cook, and to care for him, while a woman needed a man to provide her with food and clothing. Many of the older persons in both the communities have been married several times. When a spouse died, the surviving spouse frequently remarried and, as the second

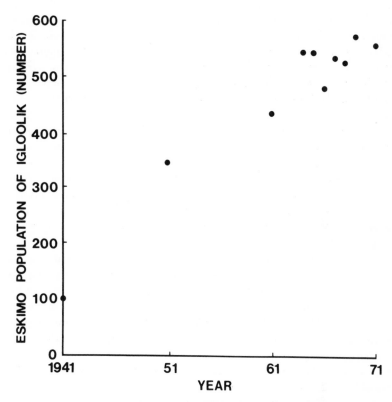

FIG. 8.   Population size of Igloolik from 1941 to 1971.

spouse also might have been married previously, families consisting of three or four half sibships were not unusual. As in the past, arranged marriages still are quite common and often the intended are promised to each other from birth. At the present time particularly in Igloolik, young persons appear to be postponing marriages because quite a number of them have spent time outside of the communities at residential schools. In Hall Beach, females are giving birth to their first child at an earlier age than their counterparts in Igloolik. This may well be a consequence of the earlier mean age of menarche of premenopausal mothers in Hall Beach as compared to Igloolik.

To date it has not been possible to determine whether the earlier age of menarche of premenopausal mothers in Hall Beach is a statistical artefact or whether it has a biological basis. Possible determinants of menarchial age have been reported to be nutrition, disease, rurality, altitude, a genetic component (Hiernaux, 1968) and height and weight (Frisch and Revelle, 1971). It is hoped that when additional data from the entire Igloolik—Hall Beach IBP project becomes available, further analyses may throw light on a possible factor or factors which may influence the age of menarche in Igloolik and Hall Beach. The mean ages of menarche of 62 premenopausal mothers in Igloolik (14.3± 0.2 yr) and of 31 in Hall Beach (13.4± 0.2 yr) are comparable to the corresponding estimate of 13.8 ± 0.8 years for Eskimos from Wainwright, Alaska (Milan, 1970). In addition, the mean age at menarche of premenopausal women in Igloolik is similar to the mean age of menarche of 14.4 ± 1.2 years of 120 Eskimos from Pt. Barrow, Alaska (Levine, 1953). However, the mean age of the Hall Beach premenopausal mothers is less than that of the Pt. Barrow females. The mean age of menarche of 16 women from Bethel, Alaska was reported to be 13.3 years (Hrdlička, 1936).

The average ages at the birth of the first child of both the 62 premenopausal mothers in Igloolik (17.9 ± 0.3 yr) and the 31 premenopausal mothers in Hall Beach (16.9 ± 0.2 yr) are lower (t = 3.30, p<0.01 and t = 4.30, p<0.01) than the mean age of 19.9 ± 0.6 years of 39 women from Wainwright (Milan, 1970). Igloolik and Hall Beach premenopausal mothers appear to have their first child sooner after menarche than do the Wainwright women. Among Igloolik premenopausal mothers the difference between the mean menarchial age and the mean age at the birth of the first child was 3.6 years, while among the Hall Beach premenopausal mothers, this difference was 3.5 years. In Wainwright the interval between the mean menarchial age and mean age at the birth of the first child was 5.1 years. Milan (1970) suggested that the non-child bearing interval following menarche in the Wainwright women may have been due to a postpubertal anovulatory period or to *coitus interruptus* as a contraceptive measure. If a postpubertal anovulatory period is an underlying factor, it must have been shorter in the Igloolik and Hall Beach premenopausal mothers than in the Wainwright women.

The distributions of livebirths and stillbirths of Igloolik and Hall Beach mothers were similar. The numbers of fetuses reported by the Igloolik mothers (7.7%) and the Hall Beach mothers (13.2%) as abortuses are similar to the reported frequency of 10.2% (37 out of 373 fetuses) reported by Eskimo women in Wainwright, Alaska. In addition, frequencies of stillbirths in Igloolik (3.4%) and in Hall Beach (2.2%) also are comparable to the 2.1% (7 out of 336) reported by Wainwright women (Milan, 1970).

Approximately 25% of all liveborn fetuses of the Igloolik and Hall Beach mothers died before 15 years of age. The fewer infant/childhood deaths reported by the Hall Beach premenopausal mothers as compared to both the artificially and the naturally postreproductive women in their community may reflect differences in the delivery of health care to these different groups of women. The women in whom sterility was induced may have had higher risks of giving birth to children who did not survive with the limited health care available than did the premenopausal mothers. As the naturally postreproductive women gave birth to the majority of their children while they still lived in camps, the health care available for these women was more limited than that provided for the premenopausal women who gave birth to the majority of their children after moving into the settlements, each of which had a nursing station. However, the numbers in the different categories are small so that the differences found may be due to spurious sampling. No differences in infant/childhood mortality rates were found when the Igloolik data were compared by the mothers' reproductive categories.

No differences in sex ratios of livebirths were found between Igloolik and Hall Beach. The proportion of the sexes of liveborn infants at birth for Igloolik and Hall Beach combined was 1.11 (419 males:379 females) which does not differ statistically from the sex ratio of 1.08 of livebirths of Eskimo women in Wainwright, Alaska (Milan, 1970).

The birth rates based on the 12 month interval prior to each field expedition were 51.4 and 36.3 per thousand population in Igloolik and Hall Beach respectively. Although insufficient data were available for calculating birth rates over a longer period of time, the 1971 birth rates for Igloolik and Hall Beach are similar to those for other Eskimo groups: 53 per thousand in the Bethel region of Alaska (Maynard, 1967) and 50.2 per thousand in all of Greenland in 1961 (Bech, 1963), although they are greatly increased over the national average of 17.6 (livebirths plus stillbirths over 28 weeks gestation) per thousand population for all of Canada in 1970 (Statistics Canada, 1970).

The frequency of reported multiple births amongst the Igloolik and Hall Beach Eskimos of 11.7 sets of multiple births per thousand births (live and stillbirths) is not statistically different from the corresponding estimate of 24.1 per thousand births for the Alaskan Eskimos from Wainwright (Milan, 1970). The estimated frequency of multiple births in Igloolik and Hall Beach is similar to the corresponding incidence of 9.99 per thousand births for all of Canada (Statistics Canada, 1970). Since numbers were small for the three Eskimo samples and there were no statistical differences between them, the data for Igloolik, Hall Beach and Wainwright were pooled and gave a multiple birth rate for Eskimos of 16.3 per thousand live and stillbirths. The multiple birth rate for Eskimos may be higher than that for North Americans in general; a comparison of 16.3 with 9.9 for all of Canada gave a χ^2 of 5.7913 for 1 df, p = 0.02.

The mean birth weight of $3.12 \pm .04$ kg for Igloolik Eskimos is below the average of 3.29 kg for all of Canada excluding Newfoundland (Statistics Canada, 1970); whether this difference is due to ethnic and/or nutritional differences is uncertain.

The average family sizes of naturally postreproductive mothers in the two communities were similar. The mean numbers of pregnancies experienced by postmenopausal women in this study were calculated so that the family data presented here (number of livebirths plus stillbirths) could be compared with those reported by Milan (1970). The 118 pregnancies experienced by the 11 Igloolik naturally postmenopausal mothers (mean 10.7 ± 0.7) and the 54 pregnancies experienced by all the Hall Beach postreproductive mothers (mean 12.8 ± 1.6) are comparable to the 159 pregnancies reported by the 17 postmenopausal women from Wainwright (mean 9.9 ± 1.0). It is too early to determine whether or not there has been a change in family size with the urbanization of the Eskimos in Igloolik and Hall Beach.

The mean age at menopause of all the naturally postreproductive women in the sample (51.5 ± 0.9 yr) was significantly greater than the mean of 44.5 ± 1.1 yr for Wainwright women reported by Milan (1970) (t = 4.954, p<0.001). The natural reproductive span of females which ranged from 28 to 43 years in the Igloolik-Hall Beach data is comparable to the span of 23 to 40 years of Wainwright females (Milan, 1970). Thus, it appears that naturally postreproductive Eskimo women from the eastern Canadian Arctic and from Alaska experience similar numbers of pregnancies over comparable reproductive spans.

Although the numbers in each category are small, the artificially postreproductive women in Hall Beach reported significantly more livebirths plus stillbirths, on the average, than did their counterparts in Igloolik. If this difference has biological significance, presumably it reflects the mean age at which sterility was induced in each group: in Hall Beach, 35.8 ± 2.9 years (range: 29-43 years), in Igloolik, 26.8 ± 2.2 years (range: 20-33 years).

No differences in child spacing between Igloolik and Hall Beach were found when the data were partitioned according to the mothers' present reproductive category. Premenopausal women had another child sooner when the index birth, whether male or female, lived less than a year than when it survived for at least a year. This may reflect the couples' desire to replace their deceased child and as the mother no longer has a child to breast feed, unless she adopts a baby from another mother, her period of natural infertility while lactating may be shortened. When the index birth lived for more than one year, the premenopausal mothers had another child sooner when the index birth was a male than when it was a female. However, if the index birth lived for less than one year, male children were replaced as soon as female children. No such differences in child spacing according to the outcome of the previous birth could be demonstrated for the naturally postreproductive mothers; whether this is a real observation or a reflection of the small numbers in some of the categories cannot be determined from these data. If the index birth lived for more than a year, the premenopausal mothers, on the average, had another child sooner than did the naturally postmenopausal mothers. This difference may be a reflection of the decreased period of breastfeeding practised by premenopausal mothers as opposed to postmenopausal mothers. Hildes and Schaefer (1973) have reported that in Igloolik older mothers did, in fact, breastfeed their children for longer periods of time than the younger women. As the use of oral contraceptives did not appear to be either widespread or effective, it probably had little effect on either family size or child spacing.

The estimate of the inbreeding coefficient of 0.001 in the Igloolik population may be underestimated as it usually was not possible to trace the genealogies back for more than four or five generations and consequently some consanguineous relationships may not have been detected. However, marrying relatives does not appear to have been a social custom in the area so perhaps the coefficient of inbreeding would not be greatly increased over that for a large random mating population. Despite the separation of Igloolik and Hall Beach from other communities by great distances there appears to have been a constant mixing of the Eskimos from neighboring areas. For example, the Igloolik people were in contact with the people from Hall Beach, and from Pond Inlet on Baffin Island, and to a lesser extent with the people from Repulse Bay. The Hall Beach people maintained regular contact with the people from Igloolik as well as from Repulse Bay and Coral Harbour. Within the last two hundred years, the Eskimos also have been in limited contact with non-Eskimos. The estimates of Caucasian admixture of about 3% in Igloolik and about 4% in Hall Beach based on interview data may be underestimates of the proportion of the gene pool in each community that is Caucasoid, as the genetic marker studies indicated that this estimate in Igloolik was approximately 7% (McAlpine et al. 1974). The lower estimate of Caucasian admixture based on the interview data may reflect reluctance on the part of the interviewee to reveal this information.

138

ACKNOWLEDGEMENTS

This study constituted part of the Canadian Human Adaptability section of the International Biological Programme (IBP), directed by Dr. D. R. Hughes, Department of Anthropology, University of Toronto. Mrs. Carol McKeen and the Department of Computer Science at Queen's University provided invaluable assistance with the computing. The Health and Welfare Division of Statistics Canada, Ottawa, provided access to recorded vital statistics. Financial assistance was provided by the Canadian Committee of the International Biological Programme and by the Medical Research Council of Canada with operating grant MT1876 to NES. PJM held a postdoctoral fellowship from the Medical Research Council of Canada.

Received: 13 May 1975.

LITERATURE CITED

BECH, V. 1963 Sundhestilstanden i Grønland. Landslaegens årsberetning 1961 Syndgrønlands Bogtrykkeri. Cited by Milan (1970).

FRISCH, R. E. AND R. REVELLE 1971 The height and weight of girls and boys at the time of the initiation of the adolescent growth spurt in height and weight and the relationship to menarche. Hum. Biol. 43: 140-159.

HIERNAUX, J. 1968 Ethnic differences in growth and development. Eugenics Quarterly 15: 12-21.

HILDES, J. A. AND O. SCHAEFER 1973 Health of Igloolik Eskimos and changes with urbanization. J. Hum. Evol. 2: 241-246.

HRDLIČKA, A. 1936 Puberty in Eskimo girls. Proc. Nat. Acad. Sci. 22: 355-357.

LEVINE, V.E. 1953 Studies in physical anthropology, III. The age of onset of menstruation of the Alaskan Eskimos. Amer. J. Phys. Anthrop. 11: 252.

MAYNARD, J. 1967 Eskimo infant deaths twice Indians. Medical Tribune Feb.: 25-26.

MCALPINE, P. J., S.-H. CHEN, D. W. COX, J. B. DOSSETOR, E. R. GIBLETT, A. G. STEINBERG AND N. E. SIMPSON 1974 Genetic markers in blood in a Canadian Eskimo population with a comparison of allele frequencies in circumpolar populations. Hum. Hered. 24: 114-142.

MILAN, F. 1970 The demography of an Alaskan Eskimo village. Arctic Anthrop. 7: 26-43.

STATISTICS CANADA 1941 Census of Canada

STATISTICS CANADA 1951 Census of Canada

STATISTICS CANADA 1956 Census of Canada

STATISTICS CANADA 1961 Census of Canada

STATISTICS CANADA 1966 Census of Canada

STATISTICS CANADA 1970 Vital Statistics in Canada

STATISTICS CANADA 1971 Census of Canada

STERN, C. 1960 Principles of human genetics. W. H. Freeman and Co., San Francisco and London. pp. 376-378.

Effects of Consanguineous Marriage and Inbreeding on Couple Fertility and Offspring Mortality in Rural Sri Lanka[1]

By Russell M. Reid[2]

ABSTRACT

A sample of 455 couples of the Goyigama Caste of rural Sri Lanka (Ceylon) were interviewed for information on consanguinity, fertility, offspring mortality, and socio-economic status. Multiple regression of various measures of fertility on the coefficient of kinship as well as temporal and socio-economic variables were performed for all couples and for those in which the wife was born after 1920. In contrast to earlier studies the consanguinity of couples was found to depress the total number of pregnancies, live births, and living offspring. All three were significantly depressed in the sample of wives born after 1920, while only the depression of the number of living offspring was significant in the total sample. Consanguinity of the couples was not found to significantly affect rates of spontaneous abortions, stillbirths, or later offspring deaths.

Theoretical population genetics predicts that for a closed population at or near genetic equilibrium, inbreeding will lower Darwinian fitness. This is because polymorphisms tend to persist if heterozygotes have the highest fitness and to move toward fixation of one of the alleles if they do not. Likewise, experience with agricultural crops and laboratory animals has led us to expect heterosis or hybred vigor for fitness. Thus, it was not surprising that studies of inbreeding in human populations in Japan (Schull and Neel, 1962, 1965, 1966; Schull et al. 1970b; Neel and Schull, 1962; Yamaguchi et al. 1970), India (Reid, 1971), Brazil (Marcallo et al. 1964), Egyptian Nubia (Hussien, 1971), Czechoslovakia (Seemánová, 1971), and Sweden (Böök, 1957) all found elevated levels of prereproductive mortality among the offspring of consanguineous couples. What was surprising, however, was the observation of elevated birth rates among consanguineous couples in studies in Japan (Schull et al. 1970a), India (Reid, 1971), Egyptian Nubia (Hussien, 1971), and among French Canadians (Philippe, 1974). Additionally, the studies of Kurdistan Jews (Goldschmidt et al. 1963) and Sweden (Böök, 1957) showed reduced frequencies of fetal loss in consanguineous couples as compared to nonconsanguineous couples of their own population. Generally, though not always, the effects on birth rates and fetal loss have not been statistically significant.

[1]Supported by NSF-USDP-1598.
[2]Department of Anthropology, University of Texas, Austin, Texas 78712.

While Schull and his associates (Schull et al. 1970a; Schull and Neel, 1972) account for the elevated fertility of consanguineous couples in Japan as a compensation for the higher mortality rates of their inbred offspring; I have speculated that in South India the fertility differences might reflect the constrasting social and psychological quality of the relations between consanguineous couples as opposed to nonconsanguineous couples (Reid, 1971). The latter are often total strangers before their marriage. In his recent study of French Canadians, Philippe (1974) suggests a reduction in the period of amenorrhea as a factor contributing to the increased fertility of cansanguineous couples.

The present paper is based on a field survey conducted by the author in Sri Lanka (Ceylon) during the summer of 1973. The survey was intended as a pilot project with several goals including: 1. an evaluation of the level of inbreeding in a rural population in Sri Lanka, 2) a test of the feasibility of collecting sensitive demographic data in a population with few documentary sources for data verification, and 3) a replication of the earlier observations on couple fertility and fetal loss in relation to parental consanguinity. It is this final goal which will be dealt with here. As with much of the research on inbreeding effects, this author's earlier work in India (Reid, 1971) made no adjustments for possible socio-economic factors that might distort the effects of consanguinity on fertility. The present study seeks to overcome this shortcoming.

MATERIALS AND METHODS

With the assistance of an interpreter, 455 couples of all ages were interviewed in various villages in the Metta Dumbara Division about 25 km east of the city of Kandy in central Sri Lanka (Ceylon). This general region has been the site for a number of important ethnographic studies (Yalman, 1971, for example). All of the couples interviewed were Goyigamas, a high caste of Sinhalese-speaking Buddhists. The Goyigamas are traditionally thought of as a caste of land-owning cultivators from which the ancient royalty came, however the survey population also included landless laborers, craftsmen, bureaucrats, merchants, and educators. The data included information on education, literacy, occupation, property holdings, previous marriages as well as the date and place of birth for both the husband and wife. Additionally, for each couple their year of marriage, nature of any consanguineous ties, and their reproductive history was recorded. In the latter I attempted to include all pregnancies and to give birth dates and vital status of all offspring. Whenever possible birthdates were verified by records, usually horoscopes. From these data the coefficient of consanguinity (see Crow and Kimura, 1970, pp. 68-69) was calculated for each couple and the mean coefficient of inbreeding was calculated for the offspring. Then a variety of measures of fertility were regressed on the couples' coefficient of consanguinity and all available temporal and socio-economic variables. This was performed by the forward multiple regression in SPSS (Nie et al. 1970), for those couples with no missing data.

RESULTS

The closest reported genealogical relationship for each couple is summarized in Table 1. While the total frequency of first cousin marriage is about the same as that I described for the Telaga-Kapu caste in southern India, (Reid, 1973a), the Indian data included closer marriages (those between a man and his sister's daughter) and fewer distant marriages. The mean inbreeding coefficient for the Sinhalese offspring is estimated as just over one percent, putting it in the upper range described for human populations (Reid, 1973b).

For each couple the following measures of fertility were examined:

1. Number of Pregnancies
2. Number of live births
3. Number of living offspring

and for couples with at least one pregnancy

4. Abortion rate (Abortions ÷ Pregnancies)
5. Stillbirth rate (Stillbirths ÷ Pregnancies)
6. Child death rate (Deaths ÷ Pregnancies)

All of the reported abortions were spontaneous. Each of these measures was then used as the dependent variable in a forward multiple regression with the following independent variables:

1. Coefficient of kinship of the couple
2. Year of Marriage and its square

3 and 4. Wife's and Husband's birth years and their squares

5 and 6. Years of education of wife and husband

7 and 8. Number of languages read by wife and husband

9 and 10. Acres of land owned by wife and husband

11 and 12. Number of previous marriages of wife and husband

The major contributing variables to the multiple regressions were consistently the year of marriage, the variables dealing with the wife and, occasionally, the coefficient of kinship. The variables dealing with the

Table 1

Distribution of closest reported Genealogical Relationship between Husband and Wife

Genealogical Relationship	Number Reported	Frequency %
MBD	42	9.2
FZD	23	5.1
MZDD or FMBD	.2	.4
2nd cousin	41	9.0
More Distant	29	6.4
Not Related	318	69.9
Total	455	100.0

M = Mother; F = Father; Z = Sister; B = Brother; D = Daughter

husband were highly correlated with those of the wife, but slightly less correlated with fertility than those of the wife. They, therefore, had little independent contribution to the multiple regressions. Because the number of pregnancies of a woman increases asymptotically with age rather than linearly, this analysis is distorted for older couples. Therefore, the same analysis was run for those couples in which the wife was born after 1920 (53 years old or less at the time of the survey). The partial regression coefficients of fertility on the coefficient of kinship are shown in Tables 2 and 3.

Among the 86 couples for whom the wife was born in the 1920's there were means of $7.407 \pm .340$ reported pregnancies, $7.163 \pm .332$ reported live births, and $6.012 \pm .297$ living offspring. These are an indication of completed family sizes for couples. They do not include additional pregnancies, etc. from other marriages of the women. The difference between the mean numbers of pregnancies and live births is clearly too small and indicates considerable underenumeration of fetal loss. The difference between numbers of live births and numbers of living offspring is more difficult to evaluate. It indicates an accumulated attrition over the years of 16% of the live born offspring. Sri Lanka has been in a period of rapid demographic transition throughout the life span of most of those offspring. Death rates have long been well below those elsewhere in South Asia, and since 1945 they have dropped very rapidly. For two decades before the collection of this data the crude death rate nation wide remained at or below 11 per thousand population per year (Abhayaratne and Jayewardene, 1967).

Table 2

Partial Regression Coefficients of Fertility Measures on the Kinship Coefficient (Other Variables are listed in the Text) for couples of all ages

Measure of Fertility	Partial Regression On Kinship	Significance Level (2-Tailed)	Multiple R
All Couples (N = 392)			
No. of Pregnancies	−6.501 ± 5.948	n.s.	.67
No. of Live Births	−8.216 ± 5.768	n.s.	.68
No. of living Children	−11.292 ± 5.395	.05	.60
Couples with at least one pregnancy (N = 372)			
Abortion Rate	.231 ± .153	n.s.	.20
Stillbirth Rate	.036 ± .286	n.s.	.14
Child Death Rate	.529 ± .421	n.s.	.52

n.s. = not significant

Table 3

Partial Regression Coefficients of Fertility Measures on the Kinship Coefficient (Other Variables are listed in the Text) for Couples in which the Wife was Born after 1920

Measures of Fertility	Partial Regression On Kinship	Significance Levels (2-Tailed)	Multiple R
Wives born after 1920 (N = 295)			
No. of Pregnancies	−13.392 ± 5.748	.025	.80
No. of Live Births	−14.937 ± 5.628	.01	.80
No. of living Children	−14.644 ± 5.213	.005	.76
Wives born after 1920 with at least one pregnancy (N = 275)			
Abortion Rate	.280 ± .209	n.s.	.21
Stillbirth Rate	.017 ± .365	n.s.	.18
Child Death Rate	.303 ± .374	n.s.	.41

n.s. = not significant

I see no reason to suspect that these data significantly underenumerate either the deaths to live born offspring or the total numbers of live births.

Two general observations can be made about these results. First, none of the measures of fertility attrition (rates of abortion, stillbirth, and death) has a significant regression on kinship. This contrasts with the significant increase in mortality associated with inbreeding in earlier studies. Second, contrary to the direction reported in previous studies, all of the positive measures of fertility (pregnancies, live births, and living offspring) regress negatively on degree of kinship. Here we see that when all couples for which there is no missing data (Table 2) are included in the analysis, only the regression of living offspring is significant. When the couples with wives born before 1920 are excluded to improve linearity, all three of these positive measures of fertility regress significantly on the kinship coefficient. This is also true when the 20 couples who report no pregnancies are excluded from the analysis (not shown here). The improved linearity in the restricted sample can be seen in the marked increase in the multiple R's for the positive measures of fertility. In short, while earlier studies have shown increased couple fertility and decreased offspring viability to be associated with parental consanguinity, these data show decreased couple fertility and no significant decrease in offspring viability. The magnitude of the partial regressions suggest that among couples with a wife born after 1920, those related as first cousins average .837 fewer pregnancies, .934 fewer live births, and .915 fewer living offspring than the average for comparable but non-consanguineous couples. These values are calculated by multiplying the partial regressions by 0.0625, the kinship coefficient of first cousins.

DISCUSSION

Direct comparison with the ethnographically similar case in southern India (Reid, 1971) is impossible, because comparable socio-economic data were not collected in the earlier study. The absence of elevated fertility (indeed the depressed fertility) in the present data is not in conflict with Schull's hypothesis of compensation, since there is no significant elevation in mortality of inbred offspring to be compensated. Further, the contrast between the present data from Sri Lanka and that from Japan (Schull et al. 1970a,b, 1972) suggest that whereas the natural selection detected by inbreeding in Japan operates primarily post-natally, it operates at the level of fertilization, and early embryological development in the Sri Lanka population. Thus, the lower reported fertility levels of the consanguineous couples. This result remains consistent with the belief that inbreeding reduces Darwinian fitness.

The effect of excluding older couples from the analysis (about one fourth of the total sample) is also noteworthy. I do not interpret the effects of that exclusion as an indication that inbreeding had different effects on older than on younger couples. Rather, that the linear regressions of numbers of pregnancies and births (and to a lesser extent the number of living offspring) on parents' years of birth and marriage are inappropriate over the total age range of the sample. A first order linear model (straight line) would overestimate the fertility of older couples while a second order linear model (parabola) might underestimate it. This would create a considerable amount of residual variance in the upper age ranges, thus the lower multiple r and higher standard errors in the total sample. By excluding older couples the sample was limited to an age range in which numbers of births and pregnancies more closely approximate a linear relationship with age and duration of marriage. This leaves less residual variance to be accounted for by the coefficient of kinship, lower standard errors, and thus more significant regressions.

Received: 8 April 1975.

LITERATURE CITED

ABHAYARATNE, O. E. R. AND C. H. S. JAYEWARDENE 1967 Fertility trends in Ceylon. Colombo.

BÖÖK, J. A. 1957 Genetical investigations in a north Swedish population: offspring of first-cousin marriages. Ann. Human Genet. 21: 191-208.

CROW, J. F. AND M. KIMURA 1970 An introduction to population genetics theory. Harper and Row, New York.

GOLDSCHMIDT, E., T. COHEN, N. BLOCH, L. KELETI AND S. WARTSKI 1963 Viability studies in Jews from Kuridstan. *In* E. Goldschmidt (ed), The genetics of migrant and isolate populations. Williams and Wilkins, New York.

HUSSIEN, F. H. 1971 Endogamy in Egyptian Nubia. J. Biosocial Sciences 3: 251-257.

MARCALLO, F. A., N. FREIRE-MAIA, J. B. C. AZEVEDO AND I. A. SIMOES 1964 Inbreeding effects on mortality and morbidity in South Brazilian populations. Ann. Human Genet. 27: 203-18.

NEEL, J. V. AND W. J. SCHULL 1962 The effect of inbreeding on mortality and morbidity in two Japanese cities. Proc. Nat. Acad. Sci. 48: 573-582.

NIE, N. H., D. H. BENT AND C. H. HULL 1970 Statistical package for the social sciences (SPSS). McGraw-Hill, New York.

PHILIPPE, P. 1974 Amenorrhea, intrauterine mortality and parental consanguinity in an isolated French Canadian population. Human Biol. 46: 405-424.

REID, R. M. 1971 Marriage patterns, demography, and population genetics in a South Indian caste: study of inbreeding in a human population. Ph.D. dissertation, University of Illinois at Urbana-Champaign.

——— 1973a Social Structure and inbreeding in a South Indian caste. *In* N. E. Morton

Russell M. Reid

(ed), Genetic structure of populations. Population genetics monographs. Volume III. University of Hawaii, Honolulu.

———— 1973b   Inbreeding in human populations. *In* M. H. Crawford and P. L. Workman (eds), Methods and theories of anthropological genetics. University of New Mexico Press, Albuquerque.

SCHULL, W. J., T. FURUSHO, M. YAMAMOTO, H. NAGANO AND I. KOMATSU   1970a   The effects of parental consanguinity and inbreeding in Hirado, Japan, IV. Fertility and reproductive compensation. Humangenetik **9:** 394-415.

SCHULL, W. J., H. NAGANO, M. YAMAMOTO AND I. KOMATSU   1970b   The effects of parental consanguinity and inbreeding in Hirado, Japan, I. Stillbirths and pre-reproductive mortality. Am. J. Human Genetics **22:** 239-262.

SCHULL, W. J. AND J. V. NEEL   1962   The effects of inbreeding on mortality and morbidity in two Japanese cities. Proc. Nat. Acad. Sci. **48:** 573-582.

———— 1965   The effects of inbreeding on Japanese children. Harper and Row, New York.

———— 1966   Some further observations on the effects of inbreeding on mortality in Kure, Japan. Am. J. Human Genet. **18:** 144-152.

———— 1972   The effects of parental consanguinity and inbreeding in Hirado, Japan. V. Summary and interpretation. Am. J. Human Genet. **27:** 425-453.

SEEMÁNOVÁ, E.   1971   A study of children of incestuous mating. Human Heredity **21:** 108-128.

YALMAN, N.   1971   Under the Bo tree: studies in caste, kinship, and marriage in the interior of Ceylon. University of California Press.

YAMAGUCHI, M., T. YANASE, H. NAGANO AND N. NAKAMOTO   1970   Effects of inbreeding on mortality in Fukuoka population. Am. J. Human Genet. **22:** 145-159.